Violence

Other books in the Social Issues Firsthand series:

Abortion

Adoption

Capital Punishment

Death and Dying

Drug Abuse

Family Violence

Gambling

Hate Crimes

Homosexuality

Immigration

Interracial Relationships

Poverty

Prisons

Racism

Religion

Suicide

Terrorism

Violence

Doreen Piano, Book Editor

GREENHAVEN PRESS
A part of Gale, Cengage Learning

GALE
CENGAGE Learning

Detroit • New York • San Francisco • New Haven, Conn • Waterville, Maine • London

GALE
CENGAGE Learning™

Christine Nasso, *Publisher*
Elizabeth Des Chenes, *Managing Editor*

© 2007 Greenhaven Press, a part of Gale, Cengage Learning.

For more information, contact:
Greenhaven Press
27500 Drake Rd.
Farmington Hills, MI 48331-3535
Or you can visit our Internet site at gale.cengage.com

LIBRARY OF CONGRESS CATALOGING-IN-PUBLICATION DATA

Violence / Doreen Piano, book editor.
    p. cm. -- (Social issues firsthand)
  Includes bibliographical references and index.
  ISBN-13: 978-0-7377-2909-2 (hardcover)
  ISBN-10: 0-7377-2909-0 (hardcover)
  1. Violence--United States. 2. Youth and violence--United States. 3. School
violence--United States. 4. United States--Social conditions. I. Piano, Doreen.
  HN90.V5V5312 2008
  306.0973--dc22
                                                                    2007020695

Printed in the United States of America
2 3 4 5 6 7 12 11 10 09 08

Contents

Foreword   **9**

Introduction   **12**

Chapter 1: Violence and Everyday Life

1. Learning How to Handle Conflict   **18**
   in the South Bronx
   Geoffrey Canada

   Witnessing his inner-city mentor's interactions, a young
   man begins to understand how breaking the implicit
   rules of the street will lead to violence.

2. Standing Up to School Violence   **29**
   Elizabeth Rusch

   A third grader in Tucson organizes an anti-violence protest at the high school across from her elementary school.

3. Harassed for Being Different   **32**
   Rhee Gold

   A man reflects on his youth as a dancer and the harassment he was subjected to by his male peers.

4. I Hate Everyone Not Like Me   **36**
   Storm Trooper Steve

   A self-identified skinhead conveys his hatred for non-
   white, non-Christian groups.

Chapter 2: Perpetrating Violence

1. My Dad Helped Me Confront a Bully   **41**
   Mikel Jollett

   A high school nerd stands up to a school bully after
   learning a lesson from his father that he would never
   learn in school.

2. I Killed My Father   **47**
   Mark

   Witness and victim to his father's rage, a teenager nar-
   rates how and why he killed his father.

3. Understanding Violence as Fantasy   **51**
Jane Katch
A teacher attempts to understand the meaning of a student's obsession with violence.

Chapter 3: Survivors and Witnesses of Violence

1. Witnessing School Violence   **55**
Melissa Miller and Cate Baily
A survivor of the Columbine High School shooting recreates her experience of that fatal day.

2. A Prisoner's Violent Death   **59**
Jean Carbone
A physician's assistant recounts her attempt and failure to save a prisoner's life.

3. My Child Was Murdered   **64**
Miriam, as told my Judie Bucholz
A mother describes the murder of her son Raymond and the subsequent grieving process.

4. I Was the Scene of a Crime   **70**
Nancy Venable Raine
A woman provides a detailed account of her experience in the hospital in the immediate aftermath of a rape.

Chapter 4: Retribution, Renunciation, and Forgiveness

1. Meeting My Sister's Murderer   **80**
Ron Carlson, as told by Rachel King
The brother of a murder victim explains how he got to know his sister's killer before she was executed in Texas in 1998.

2. A Friend of Mine Was Raped   **91**
Gerald, as told by Charlotte Pierce-Baker
After hearing his friend tell him that she was the victim of acquaintance rape, a young man understands he is capable of bringing greater awareness of sexual violence to his community.

3. A Death Row Convict Writes to Help Others   **99**
   Vince Beiser

   A death row inmate edits a bimonthly prison literary
   magazine and uses the money the magazine earns to
   hand out scholarships to family members of homicide
   victims.

4. After Constantine's Death, I Wanted His   **102**
   Murderer to Die
   Olga Polites

   After a relative's brutal murder, the author reflects on
   why she can no longer be opposed to the death penalty.

Organizations to Contact   **105**

For Further Research   **112**

Index   **115**

Foreword

Social issues are often viewed in abstract terms. Pressing challenges such as poverty, homelessness, and addiction are viewed as problems to be defined and solved. Politicians, social scientists, and other experts engage in debates about the extent of the problems, their causes, and how best to remedy them. Often overlooked in these discussions is the human dimension of the issue. Behind every policy debate over poverty, homelessness, and substance abuse, for example, are real people struggling to make ends meet, to survive life on the streets, and to overcome addiction to drugs and alcohol. Their stories are ubiquitous and compelling. They are the stories of everyday people—perhaps your own family members or friends—and yet they rarely influence the debates taking place in state capitols, the national Congress, or the courts.

The disparity between the public debate and private experience of social issues is well illustrated by looking at the topic of poverty. Each year the U.S. Census Bureau establishes a poverty threshold. A household with an income below the threshold is defined as poor, while a household with an income above the threshold is considered able to live on a basic subsistence level. For example, in 2003 a family of two was considered poor if its income was less than $12,015; a family of four was defined as poor if its income was less than $18,810. Based on this system, the bureau estimates that 35.9 million Americans (12.5 percent of the population) lived below the poverty line in 2003, including 12.9 million children below the age of eighteen.

Commentators disagree about what these statistics mean. Social activists insist that the huge number of officially poor Americans translates into human suffering. Even many families that have incomes above the threshold, they maintain, are likely to be struggling to get by. Other commentators insist that the statistics exaggerate the problem of poverty in the United States. Compared to people in developing countries, they point out, most so-called poor families have a high quality of life. As stated by journalist Fidelis Iyebote, "Cars are owned by 70 percent of 'poor' households. . . . Color televisions belong to 97 percent of the 'poor' [and] videocassette recorders belong to nearly 75 percent. . . . Sixty-four percent have microwave ovens, half own a stereo system, and over a quarter possess an automatic dishwasher."

However, this debate over the poverty threshold and what it means is likely irrelevant to a person living in poverty. Simply put, poor people do not need the government to tell them whether they are poor. They can see it in the stack of bills they cannot pay. They are aware of it when they are forced to choose between paying rent or buying food for their children. They become painfully conscious of it when they lose their homes and are forced to live in their cars or on the streets. Indeed, the written stories of poor people define the meaning of poverty more vividly than a government bureaucracy could ever hope to. Narratives composed by the poor describe losing jobs due to injury or mental illness, depict horrific tales of childhood abuse and spousal violence, recount the loss of friends and family members. They evoke the slipping away of social supports and government assistance, the descent into substance abuse and addiction, the harsh realities of life on the streets. These are the perspectives on poverty that are too often omitted from discussions over the extent of the problem and how to solve it.

Greenhaven Press's Social Issues Firsthand series provides a forum for the often-overlooked human perspectives on society's most divisive topics of debate. Each volume focuses on one social issue and presents a collection of ten to sixteen narratives by those who have had personal involvement with the topic. Extra care has been taken to include a diverse range of perspectives. For example, in the volume on adoption, readers will find the stories of birth parents who have made an adoption plan, adoptive parents, and adoptees themselves. After exposure to these varied points of view, the reader will have a clearer understanding that adoption is an intense, emotional experience full of joyous highs and painful lows for all concerned.

The debate surrounding embryonic stem cell research illustrates the moral and ethical pressure that the public brings to bear on the scientific community. However, while nonexperts often criticize scientists for not considering the potential negative impact of their work, ironically the public's reaction against such discoveries can produce harmful results as well. For example, although the outcry against embryonic stem cell research in the United States has resulted in fewer embryos being destroyed, those with Parkinson's, such as actor Michael J. Fox, have argued that prohibiting the development of new stem cell lines ultimately will prevent a timely cure for the disease that is killing Fox and thousands of others.

Each book in the series contains several features that enhance its usefulness, including an in-depth introduction, an annotated table of contents, bibliographies for further research, a list of organizations to contact, and a thorough index. These elements—combined with the poignant voices of people touched by tragedy and triumph—make the Social Issues Firsthand series a valuable resource for research on today's topics of political discussion.

Introduction

Whether experienced at home, in the workplace, or at school, the United States has become a nation of witnesses and victims of violence. According to the FBI Uniform Crime Reports, an estimated 16,692 persons were murdered nationwide in 2005, an increase of 3.4 percent from 2004. Besides murder, an estimated 93,934 forcible rapes and 862,947 aggravated assaults were reported to law enforcement during 2005. When compared to the mid-1990s, violent crime has been decreasing over a ten-year period and yet research shows that violence in everyday life continues to be a social and public health problem, especially for the United States' most vulnerable populations: women, children, the poor, the incarcerated, and young men.

As this volume shows, statistics on crime do not reveal the whole story. The forms of violence that confront people daily may not be those that show up as crime statistics. Bullying, acquaintance rape, aggressive play, stalking, intimidation tactics, and domestic abuse often go unreported even though they occur in the spaces of everyday lives. These forms of violence have become naturalized; in other words, abusive behaviors appear to be normal or ordinary, even typical because violence itself has become a pervasive and sometimes unquestioned aspect of daily life.

The Everyday Spaces Where Violence Takes Place

Often it is the relatively unspectacular incidents that contribute to becoming both a victim and a perpetrator of violence. Verbal abuse such as teasing, threatening, or making derogatory comments based on race, gender, sexuality, and/or disability contributes to creating a violent environment. It is not unusual for this type of behavior to be condoned; in other words, it is not taken seriously or seen as a normal part of everyday social interaction. Taken to a physical level, these forms of abuse can lead to a serious problem among young people: bullying. Bullying has become so frequent among young children that, according to the Centers for Disease Control (CDC) Youth Violence Fact Sheet, "an estimated 30% of 6^0 to 10^0 graders in the United States were involved in bullying as a bully, a target of bullying, or both."

While the fact sheet reveals that high profile school shootings such as those occurring in Littleton, Colorado in 1999 account for less than 1% of homicides among school-aged children and youth, what is significant in the case of the Columbine shooters, Dylan Klebold and Eric Harris, was that they had been continually harassed and bullied by popular students such as the school's "jocks" and "preps." In a 1999 *New York Times* article written about the trench coat mafia, a high school clique that included Klebold and Harris, journalist Jodi Wilgoren captures an attitude that is prevalent among bullies when she writes,

> Kevin Koeniger, a 17-year-old junior on the Columbine Rebels football team, acknowledged that some athletes had teased the trench coat mafia. But, he said, the group often seemed to be asking for it.
>
> "If they're different, why wouldn't we look at them as weird?" he asked, recalling a student last year who seemed never to shower.

In a well-to-do community such as Littleton, Colorado, where school violence on the scale of the Columbine massacre was unprecedented, having the privilege to tease and bully without any repercussion reinforces social hierarchies among groups who may not have other strong distinctions such as economic and/or racial differences. Similar situations are found in the workplace and at home. The attitude expressed by the athlete—that someone's behavior asks for a certain kind of violent response because of how they look—is one prevalent in society and is often a typical response to women who have been sexually assaulted and who may dress and/or act provocatively. Blaming the victim rather than taking responsibility for living in a culture that often rewards or condones violence not only leads to more violence but it contributes to a culture of fear in which it becomes difficult to speak out as a victim.

Theories of Violence in Everyday Life

According to psychiatrist James Gilligan in his 2001 book, *Preventing Violence*, teasing and bullying can incite feelings of inadequacy and shame in those being victimized. This in turn contributes to an environment where violent behavior, especially among young men, is a permissible response because their masculinity is perceived as being under attack.

> Violence . . . is multi-determined, i.e. it is the product of the interaction between a multiplicity of biological, psychological, and social causes, or variables . . . each of which can be shown to have the effect of increasing or decreasing the frequency and severity of violence, when all the other variables are held constant. However, beneath all that there are certain regularities and unities, one of which is that shame is a necessary (but not a sufficient) cause of violence, in the same sense that the tubercle bacillus is a necessary (but not a sufficient) cause of tuberculosis.

What is interesting about Gilligan's theory is not that factors such as lack of education, mental illness, poverty, physical and sexual abuse, and social neglect may lead people to commit a violent act, it is how these factors contribute to or facilitate feelings of shame that may ultimately lead to a violent crime. In the case of the Columbine High School massacre, Klebold and Harris's violent attack on their teachers and fellow students could have been induced by their peers' harassment and bullying. More telling is that rather than discuss being harassed with school teachers, counselors, or even their parents, Klebold and Harris created numerous videotapes and a Web site to express their feelings of anger and revenge. In addition to Gilligan's theory of shame as an instrumental factor in understanding why men in particular are prone to violent behavior are feminist theories of violence that investigate how the institutions of everyday life are structured to reinforce uneven power relations between men and women.

What theories of violence illustrate is that violence is integrated into the very structure of society, a society based on unequal relations that are often times quite apparent as in the case of economic disparities between rich and poor, and men and women, and sometimes symbolic as in the case of Columbine High where difference is based on imagined social hierarchies. While preventive measures such as counseling, educational workshops, and social services may help contain violent behavior among vulnerable populations, what is truly needed is a deep restructuring of society, one that acknowledges that economic disparity is often at the root of violent behavior and criminal acts. Studies have shown that in countries where the disparity between rich and poor is low, such as Sweden and Japan, less violent behavior is evident. With this statistic in mind, it is not surprising that the United States has the highest crime rate of any other industrialized nation and its economic disparity is the most extreme.

Changing Behavior

While these statistics appear grim, there is also room for hope. As some of the articles in this volume show, if violence is a part of everyday life then perhaps people need to understand how they are implicated through everyday thoughts and behavior. How is the violent culture perpetuated and how can communities, workplaces, and schools become less tolerant of violent behavior, whether it is physical, verbal, or symbolic? With more studies concerned with mining the root causes of violence in everyday life, perhaps intolerance will grow for the injurious ways in which people behave toward each other. In other words, accepting responsibility for a violent culture may be a fundamental step toward creating a socially just society.

CHAPTER 1

Violence and Everyday Life

Learning How to Handle Conflict in the South Bronx

Geoffrey Canada

Educator, public advocate, and writer Geoffrey Canada was born in 1952 in New York City, the third of four brothers. Throughout his adult life, he has worked diligently to provide inner city children with the necessary tools to escape poverty and violence. In his coming-of-age memoir published in 1995, Fist Stick Knife Gun: A Personal History of Violence in America, *Canada depicts how the threat of violence is an everyday experience for young people in the South Bronx in New York City. Growing up in a single parent household with a mother who taught him that he had to defend himself, Canada found that the only way to survive on the streets was to learn the "codes of conduct"— implicit rules of the street that must be followed in order to avoid being a victim of violence. Although the South Bronx in the 1960s was plagued by inner city poverty, violence, and urban decay, Canada also shows how strong bonds formed between young men as a matter of survival as well as companionship. In this excerpt from his memoir, a thirteen-year-old Geoffrey learns the importance of defending one's turf and thus one's reputation by observing how his mentor Mike adamantly insists on getting his basketball back from a stranger.*

Rules ... still exist today in the ghettos across this country. If you wonder how a fourteen-year-old can shoot another child his own age in the head, or how boys can do "drive-by shootings" and then go home to dinner, you need to know you don't get there in a day, or week, or month. It takes years of preparation to be willing to commit murder, to be willing to kill or die for a corner, a color, or a leather jacket. Many of the children of America are conditioned early to kill and, more frighteningly, to die for what to an outsider might seem a trivial cause. The codes of conduct on the streets of our slums have always been hard, cold, and unforgiving. But with the influx of hundreds of thousands of handguns, you have a new brand of gunslinger among the young. Countless young people today are more dangerous than Jessie James or Billy the Kid ever were. Indeed, the Wild West was never as wild as many communities in Chicago, Los Angeles, New York, Boston (and on and on) are today. And, just as important, there's no Wyatt Earp—no one person or one program powerful enough—coming to town to clean up the mess.

It's handguns that make living in the inner city so lethal today. People have been armed and violent for a long time, but the weapon of choice used to be a bottle or a knife: the explosion of killing we see today is based on decades of ignoring the issue of violence in our inner cities. Every indicator I see suggests that it's going to get worse. How much worse? I don't think we understand the potential of how bad it can get.

A crucial part of the problem is that there are so few natural checks on killing today. This might sound strange, but while killing another person is not natural, it's not that difficult to learn. No, I've never killed anyone. But for those of you who think killing is somehow impossible to imagine, just look around the world. Wars abound—intentional starvation, the killing of civilians, women, and children—and these atrocities are sometimes committed by farmers, laborers, and other ordinary people. Even in this country the military can take an eighteen-year-old boy and turn him into a killer in a matter of months. People can be *taught* to kill. And children growing up under the conditions of war that we find in many poor communities today learn to think about death and killing as a matter of survival. And of course there are always those who are willing to teach children how to kill, and how to die.

19

These are usually the real role models in our inner cities, older boys or girls who teach the codes of conduct and enforce the rules of order.

Learning the Rules

When I was growing up in the South Bronx there were some natural checks on violent behavior. Most violence on the block was done with the fists in what we called a "fair one": two people fought until one was too hurt to continue or quit in defeat. There were people around to ensure the dispute was settled according to the rules. No "dirty" fighting was allowed, no kicking or biting, no weapons. If someone violated the rules he might be attacked or ostracized by the group. Violence against others who did not live on the block was not subject to the same rules—in these situations you could do whatever you liked—but even so, because none of us had guns, knife fighting was usually the most extreme form these encounters took. Anyone who has ever fought with a weapon like a knife or a bottle knows there is no glamour in it. These fights are messy and dangerous, even deadly. The use of weapons usually occurred only in someone else's territory.

The first rules I learned on Union Avenue stayed with me for all of my youth. They were simple and straightforward: Don't cry. Don't act afraid. Don't tell your mother. Take it like a man. Don't let no one take your manhood. My teachers were the typical instructors on blocks like Union Avenue—the adolescents we all looked up to.

It would have been only natural for me to try to emulate the boys who were two or three years older than I was, but I saw that they were still in the learning stage themselves. The group I sought out was the boys who were seven and eight years older, the group that dominated our block. We all looked up to them. They were both caring and offhandedly cruel toward us. We lived for their praise and cringed at the slightest sign of dissatisfaction. They considered us their charges to raise on the block, and our lessons were sometimes taught by the group and sometimes by individuals.

These boys were by and large just like others growing up in America's urban ghettos. They worked when they could, some struggled with school, only one had gone to college (and that was on a basketball scholarship). They hung out on the corners and stoops of the tenements and passed on the codes of conduct to those younger than themselves. This was a time before crack, so there was no money to be made hanging on the corner selling drugs. These boys were broke, with hopes and dreams but few opportunities. They took pride in what they had—"heart" and a fierce loyalty to one another and to the block. They had no clear leader, but two of them made up the center of the group, Mike and Junior. They were the best athletes, both could fight well, and they were respected on and off the block. They seemed to have conquered the fear and the anxiety of living in the ghetto, and I, like all the other boys, admired them and wanted their friendship and their protection.

But their friendship was basically unachievable for those of us who were so much younger. What we got were some brief moments to sit with them or stand near them. Maybe they would let one of us play on their side in a stickball game if they were desperate for another player. But more than likely we would be told to "get lost" when they saw us hanging around, or simply be looked at as if we had lost our minds or something when they wanted us to leave. If you were smart you left immediately. Those who did not were run off with curses, ridicule, sometimes a smack upside the head. We learned to read them like a thermometer; we knew when we could stay and when we had to leave. I was able to break into this group of older boys only because of my relationship with Mike.

Owing What I Knew to Mike

If I have accomplished anything with my life, Mike is directly responsible. He rescued me when I was a small, helpless boy, confused and scared in the South Bronx. Try as I might, I just couldn't understand the codes of conduct on Union Avenue. In fact, when I thought about the rules of the block it reminded me of looking into my older brother's math book—familiar numbers strung together in strange ways, weird signs never seen before. I realized that if you started at the beginning of the book and had the help of a good teacher you might eventually understand what those numbers and signs meant. But on the street the price for not knowing or not responding correctly was more painful than a failing grade. And one of the first things I realized was that most of the boys my age were as uninformed as I was. They learned mostly by trial and error. The older boys often talked in absolutes when they tried to pass on useful information: "Don't ever take no shit from nobody. Anybody f--- with you, bust their ass!" We would all solemnly nod our heads like we understood. But I would be thinking, "How can he say that? Everybody takes shit from somebody. We all take shit from the older guys every day."

I once tried to question the older boys, to get more clarity on what they were trying to teach us. "Well, suppose you can't *beat* the kid, then what?"

The response was pure Union Avenue. First the mocking repeat of the question in a whining, high-pitched voice: "'Well, suppose you can't *beat* the kid?' Wassa matta, nigger? You scared? You sound like a little bitch. 'Well, suppose you can't *beat* the kid?' You scared of everybody bigga than you. Alan's bigga than you, you scared of him?"

Well, I knew where this was leading. Next thing you know Alan and I would be in the street fighting to the cheers of the kids on the block, all over nothing. My response was to sit down on the curb, head down, trying to become invisible, praying for a distraction or any other salvation. Try not to cry. Please, God, don't let me cry. I learned today's lesson. Shut up. Just keep quiet.

I became friends with Mike because I loved the mornings on Union Avenue. Early in the morning Union Avenue was a peaceful place. You could walk up and down the block without the usual concern about who might tease you, or laugh at the fact that your clothes were cheap or you didn't have money for a haircut. Mike also liked to get up early. He lived on his own, in a basement apartment that we called "the cut."

Mike's mother was unable or unwilling to care for him, leaving him alone to raise himself the best way he could. Mike was everything I wanted to be—handsome, athletic, tough, and, most important to me, he was smart. He read books. And he was proud of it. With Mike I could be myself. He knew I was in the top class at P.S. 99. He knew I read adult novels in the fifth grade. And on weekend and summer mornings we talked about all kinds of subjects.

It was Mike I turned to for help in understanding Union Avenue. He was the one who told me about heart, about gaining respect, about when to fight and how. Most of all Mike was my protector. It wasn't that he fought my battles. He didn't. But when I was with him I was safe, no one would bother me. And as my friendship with Mike became known to others, the zone of safety he created for me was respected by people on and off the block. The word got out quickly: "Don't mess with him, he's Mike's boy." For me, a small boy in a mean ghetto, no father, no adult male to teach me or protect me, Mike was like a knight in shining armor.

Anything Could Happen at Any Time

The one thing you could count on in the South Bronx, though, was that any real friendship you established would be tested time and time again. You just never knew where or what the test might be.

Mike and I established a Saturday ritual. I would go to the cut and wake him up, we would get some breakfast from a local greasy spoon, and then go shoot some baskets at the local park. Mike was intent on teaching me how to play basketball and made sure I got some practice in before the real players came on the court later in the afternoon.

Well, this one morning when I was eleven, I went to the cut, woke up Mike, grabbed the ball, and went outside to wait for him. I was shooting the ball up against a parking sign. I missed the sign and hit a new car.

Now, on our block men were always yelling at us to quit leaning on their cars and new cars were fairly rare. We knew most everybody on the block and they all knew the codes of conduct. Yelling and threatening us for sitting or leaning on a car was perfectly legitimate, but that's as far as an owner could go. We, on the other hand, had to get off the car immediately when asked and act sufficiently intimidated. It wasn't lost on us that when the older boys were on the same car, there were no threats, no yelling, but even the older boys had to respect men. (Like new cars, they were fairly rare on Union Avenue.)

A man I had never seen before was coming down the block. He saw the basketball bouncing off his new car and came storming up to me. "Give me that f---ing ball!" I looked up, shocked. The menace in his voice and posture were clearly evident to me. I was scared but I had to protest. This was Mike's ball, and we all knew that you didn't let anyone take anything away from you that belonged to the older boys, especially Mike. I knew what l had to do, play the little-boy role and explain about the ball.

"Mister, this ain't my ball. This ball belongs to a boy named Mike. . . ." I never got to finish the sentence. In two steps he was right on top of me, and I could tell he was trying to decide whether my impertinence demanded a slap. I cringed. He snatched the ball from my hands.

"I don't care whose f---ing ball this is, it's mine now." It was final. The decision had been made.

The thing about the South Bronx was that you never could relax. Anything might happen at any given time. Here it was, eight o'clock on a beautiful, sunny summer morning, and my world was turned upside down. I was in a panic. Mike had told me about letting people push you around, and I had been doing a pretty good job of putting an end to people doing that to me. But what was I supposed to do about this huge man? Did Mike expect me to fight *him*? I couldn't. I was scared, and with my fear came an old companion—shame. I began to beg the man as the tears rolled down my face. "Please, mister, give me the ball. It ain't my ball. I'm gonna get in trouble. That's Mike's ball."

The man ignored me. He put the ball in his trunk, took out a rag, and began wiping off his car. I prayed he would drive off. Just leave with the ball, I'll tell Mike what happened and deal with the consequences. My prayers were not answered. Just then I saw Mike and his best friend, Junior, coming down the block toward me. I looked at the man. He was much bigger than Mike or Junior. I didn't like their odds.

The Showdown

It was Mike who spoke first. He saw my tears and with true concern asked me what was wrong. I told him that the man took his ball, my shame hot on my face. Mike didn't understand. He asked which way the man had gone. I explained that the man was right there, only five feet away, wiping down his car. Mike asked why he'd taken the ball and I told him I'd accidently hit the car.

Mike laughed. Clearly this was just a misunderstanding. He approached the man and said calmly, "Excuse me, but you have my ball." The man turned, looked Mike up and down, and said, "That's *my* ball now, and that's it."

Mike did something I would later see him do many times whenever a situation was getting out of control. He became calm and clear. He said, "Well, maybe you didn't understand me, but that's my ball, not the kid's. Mine."

This should have been all the man needed to understand that he faced a new situation. According to the codes of conduct, no man could let another man take his property, period. If you let that happen you might as well never come back on the block, for you would get no respect from anyone ever again. So Mike was letting the man know that even though he might have thought he was taking a ball from a kid, he was really taking it from another man, one who would fight to the death to defend his property. The man could give back the ball with no loss of face. But he was not from our block and he apparently didn't know the codes of conduct on the streets of the South Bronx.

"I don't give a f--- whose ball this was, it's mine now," he said. Junior moved first. He shifted over to the man's right just enough so that the man couldn't watch him and Mike at the same time. Mike took a step to the man's left. He spoke with unmistakable conviction.

"Listen, if you don't give me my ball, I'm gonna kick your f---ing ass right now all up and down this block." He took a step toward the man. Junior shifted just enough to get in a good shot. The man realized that he'd completely underestimated who he was dealing with. There was no doubt that a vicious fight was about to ensue, and the two young men he faced were not only unafraid but acting in concert in a way that conveyed that this was not the first time they had done this.

The man pulled out his car keys and took a step toward the trunk of his car. We all knew that some men carried their guns in their trunk. Things were quickly getting out of hand.

Mike's hand went into his jacket pocket, and we could all hear the click of the knife locking as he opened it quickly and efficiently with one hand. Junior put his hand inside his jacket at his neck, where I knew he often wore a chain with a combination lock on it, a dangerous weapon. Both of them stepped toward the man. If he thought he was going to scare them off he was mistaken. This was their block. They couldn't run.

I realized that this was decision time. No turning back now. Some of the swagger had gone from the man's demeanor. The trunk opened. Everyone tensed, ready for action. "Where's that jack?" he said aloud as he pulled it from the car. The situation was diffused. Mike said, "Yo, man. The ball."

"All right, here it is. I'll give it to you this time," the man said, trying to save some face.

"Yeah, I'll bet you will," Mike said, unwilling to let the man off scot-free after he'd precipitated an unnecessary crisis. The ball in hand, Mike gave it back to me and we began to walk to the park.

Afterwards, No One Said a Word

Next came what I found the most baffling part of living on Union Avenue. Nothing. I mean *nothing*. I was filled with adrenaline, questions, fear—the emotional reservoir of my mind was overflowing. But from Mike and Junior, nothing. I tried to engage them in conversation about the incident. "He was an asshole. Forget it." That was all that was said. That morning I couldn't concentrate on shooting baskets. I kept looking at Mike. He'd been willing to risk his life for a basketball. Well, not for the ball itself, but for the principle behind Union Avenue's idea of being a man. Then afterwards he acted as if it was no big deal. How could he keep his emotions so under control? How could he switch from being ready to fight to the death to making small talk about the upcoming stickball game, all within thirty seconds?

I knew that what I had just witnessed was important. Because of the unpredictability of life in the South Bronx, you had to learn how to dominate your emotions. You couldn't dwell on issues that caused fear or anger. Things happened, you acted, you moved on. If you didn't learn how to do this you might never make it out of the Bronx alive. Or if you lived you would become a slave to your emotions, ping-ponging from one to the next. The fear, the doubt, the anger, would crowd your mind until there would be no room for any of the good things—love, friendship, laughter.

Over the years I would see many people who had literally gone mad trying to survive the unpredictability and constant pressures of the Bronx. When I was growing up we used to say someone had "lost it" to explain behaviors that were due to poor mental health. What we meant was that when a person did some outrageous act that was totally out of character, he or she had "lost their mind." One day this boy Randall lost it and chased a boy we used to call B.J. down the block with a machete. Randall was such a quiet guy, never caused any trouble. B.J. said they'd just been joking around and the next thing he knew he was running for his life. Randall later seemed fine, but we never fully trusted him again.

My life in the Bronx would be a constant struggle to do what had to be done while keeping my emotions under control. Emotions got in the way of acting, and the ability to act when you had to was crucial in maintaining some control over your environment.

Learning the process of separating fear from action took years. Mike was the teacher, I the student. In a world of violence that escalated in frequency and intensity with each year he grew older, every boy needed someone to help him figure out how and when to act. Most young people did not have the advantage I did of a teacher who'd lived long enough to know that there are no absolutes, who was tough but patient. There is nothing as dangerous as advice from a thirteen-year-old on how to handle a violent confrontation. Because I hung out with Mike I learned my lessons from some of the masters, but there was a price to pay.

Standing Up to School Violence

Elizabeth Rusch

In her story about Gabriela Contreras, Elizabeth Rusch provides the reader with a glimpse of how children are confronting the increasing problem of gang violence in schools. As a third grader in Tucson, Arizona, Gabriela organized a protest against the gang violence that she and her classmates observed at the high school across the street from her school. Besides the protests, Gabriela also started a club that had a strong outreach program. Both of these actions illustrate the importance of empowering youth by getting involved in solving community problems regardless of one's age.

The gang violence had gone too far. Gabriella Contreras couldn't ignore it anymore. She had to act, and act quickly.

That was in 1996. Contreras, now 16 years old, was a third grader in Tucson, Arizona. Across the street from her school, a Special Weapons and Tactics (SWAT) team had been called to Tucson High School. The team is made up of police officers. They are trained to use special weapons. They act in a crisis.

The SWAT team had been called to break up a fight between teens. Like many other fights at the high school, this fight had to do with drugs and gangs.

The fight scared Gabriella and her classmates. They were afraid someone would get badly hurt.

Gabriella and her friends watched the SWAT team break up the fight. "I wish someone would do something to stop this," said one friend.

Gabriella replied, "Why don't we do something?"

Elizabeth Rusch, "Taking Action: She Stood Up to School Violence," *Know Your World Extra*, vol. 35, February 22, 2002, pp. 2–4. Copyright © 2002 Weekly Reader Corporation, adapted from Generation Fix: Young Ideas for a Better World by Elizabeth Rusch. Reproduced by permission of the author.

She and her friends made big signs. The signs said "Stop the Violence!" and "Make Hugs Not Drugs!"

They Stopped Fighting

The next day Gabriella and her friends marched outside their school with their signs. The high school students saw them. But they didn't stop fighting. The young students marched every day. Finally, the high school students stopped fighting.

Gabriella said, "The high school students realized that there are these little kids watching. They see what you're doing. They hear what you're saying. They see how you dress, how you act."

Gabriella and her classmates didn't want their good work to end. She wanted to start a club to help other people.

Gabriella created a club called Be Alert: Don't Do Drugs (BADDD). The club's motto is: Even as youth we can make a difference in our home, neighborhood, school, and community. More than 50 people showed up for the first meeting of Club BADD.

Club BADDD worked with food banks and clothing banks. The banks gave food and clothes to people who needed them. The club also held art shows of antidrug posters made by students.

The club gained a lot of attention. Soon students from across the country started writing Gabriella. Students wanted to know how to start their own BADDD clubs.

Making A Difference

Club BADDD is now in other Tucson schools. Gabriella and her fellow BADDD members still work hard against school violence. One peace rally in March 2000 drew more than 500 people.

Gabriella said she has learned that a person is never too young to make a difference. She has been around the United

States and Europe to get this message across. She hopes she can encourage other young people to do volunteer work.

Harassed for Being Different

Rhee Gold

For many young men who aspire to be dancers, there are social stigmas attached to this activity that may result in harassment, specially during adolescence. Rhee Gold tackles the difficulties that adolescent boys undergo when they want to be dancers by reflecting on his own fears about being bullied for being a dancer when he was young. He addresses the need for the dance community and parents to support young male dancers who may be experiencing peer pressure and even physical attacks. These young men need people to talk to and people to speak with their school principle or teachers. Unfortunately, the bullying of male dancers is often perpetuated by adults who see dance as unacceptable because it does not fit their definition of masculine behavior.

Earlier this year, I was helping a dance-teacher friend prepare a few of her dancers for a title competition. The dancers were to be scored on a talent presentation as well as a judge's interview. My job was to prepare each of the kids for the dreaded interview. This was not the first time I had done this; I have been part of more than a dozen mock interviews over the past couple of years.

The first couple of dancers—girls—went through the process smoothly. The third one was a 15-year-old boy who had trained with this particular teacher since the age of 3. I had seen him perform many times and I knew he was excellent. He's the kind of kid who always stands out, not only because he is a strong technician but because he gives the audience that "I love what I do" feeling whenever he hits the stage.

He did very well with the first few questions, as I expected from such a personable kid. Then I said, "Tell me what your male friends think about your dancing." All of a sudden there was silence. His confidence level went from one hundred to one. At first he started to ramble without really answering the question, so I asked it again. Within seconds, he was crying.

He started telling me that he didn't want to go to school anymore because he was constantly being harassed and he was actually beaten up several times—all because he danced. He said his classmates—boys and girls alike—were always calling him a fag. He was dealing with this day in and day out, and it had obviously had a major emotional effect on him.

I Told Him: Keep Dancing

Instead of continuing with the interview, I gave him a pep talk and tried to explain that the kids who were making fun of him could be jealous, or didn't comprehend how athletic dance really was. I encouraged him to keep dancing because I thought he had what it took to make it. We ended our time together with a laugh or two, but I could tell he was extremely troubled.

As I was driving home, I couldn't get this kid out of my mind. I, too, had danced from age 3 on. I had no choice: My mother was my dance teacher and my father was in show business. And I had been through the same torment this kid was enduring. I can remember sneaking out the back door of my junior high school to avoid the bullies who would think nothing of giving me a punch or two and call me a fag every time they had the opportunity.

I remember one morning when I was walking to school: I arrived at the front door wearing a winter coat with a hood. One of the kids, who I knew was trouble, walked up to me and pulled my hood off my head to spit in my face as he called me a fag. Another time, I was walking home from school and the same kid picked up a huge two-by-four and whacked me in the stomach several times as he called me unprintable names.

When I got to high school the situation was worse; like the boy in the interview, I didn't want to go to school either. But, through it all, there was never a question of whether I would continue dancing, because it was in my blood and I loved it. My issue was how I was going to keep myself from getting beaten up or from being brought down by the name-calling. Somehow, I managed.

Passing on Prejudice

When I was about 16, our family did an interview with the local newspaper. It was a story about the Gold family and how we all were into show business. Instead of being excited about my picture being in the paper, I was in fear that this article would be another opportunity to remind all the bullies that I danced. And it did. The article appeared, and so did an entirely new round of harassment.

I never talked to my parents about the situation; actually, I never discussed it with anyone for more than twenty years. I think I was embarrassed, and I didn't want anyone to know about it. Why I was embarrassed I don't know; it was just one of those things you push to the back of your mind. It was the interview with this boy that brought it all back to me—not just the memories, but the feelings as well.

You would think that the twenty-first century would bring a new perception of male dancers. They are everywhere, from Gap commercials to MTV, and they are portrayed in a very masculine way. So why are boys who dance still going through the persecution? I believe it's the adults in the kid's life who influence this kind of behavior or thinking. They are the ones I went to school with, and they still think that dancing is a "sissy" thing for guys to do. They pass their prejudices on to their children, creating an entirely new generation of kids who make fun of boys who dance.

Sticking It Out

Dance teachers and parents need to realize that their male dancers may be suffering through this torment; the kids may not bring it up because they are embarrassed, as I was. It might be a good thing to discuss at the studio or at home. It could be through rap sessions with all the dancers or one-on-one conversations with the boys. They need to know that they are not alone, that there are others who deal with the same issue. Just talking about it could make a world of difference. Another option might be for the parent and child to approach his teachers or school principal about the problem. In certain situations, counseling may be appropriate.

Often, dance teachers see young male dancers who show enormous potential and love dancing but who quit at the age of 12 or 13. My guess is that it's because they cannot take the abuse. I wonder—how many great dancers have we lost in this way?

Hard as it may be, I encourage young male dancers to stick it out. I have no regrets; I think it was the harassment that motivated me to become what I am today. Now I realize it was a unique motivation for me. I went on to perform all over the country and even became Mr. Dance of America in 1982. Today I direct one of the largest dance production companies in the world; I am a past president of Dance Masters of America; I serve as a motivational speaker for dance educators; and I write for *Dance* Magazine. Not bad for a kid who could have given it all up just to stop the torment.

By the way, the last time I saw the kid who spit in my face and hit me with the two-by-four, he was working at the local gas station.

I Hate Everyone Not Like Me

Storm Trooper Steve

While the youth subculture known as "skinheads" was originally part of a new movement among working-class white youth who identified with an emerging reggae culture known as "rude boy" in Great Britain in the late 1960s, its current manifestation in the United States is most often associated with white supremacist ideology. Knee-high military boots, shaved heads, and tattoos are a skinhead's most identifiable stylistic trait while their philosophy—that western culture is superior to all others—often manifests itself in hate crimes against people of color, gays, and Jews. As a self-pronounced skinhead, Storm Trooper Steve expresses the typical sentiments associated with white supremacy, revealing his resentment toward non-white, non-heterosexual people by vilifying and stereotyping their behavior.

When people ask me why I'm doing what I'm doing, it's so obvious. Whenever I walk around San Francisco, it's just *wham!* Now I know why I'm a skinhead, because San Francisco is so f---ing gross. I'm living in your faggot capital of the universe and I'm living it up. I'm partying it up.

But no one likes me. Everyone hates skinheads. People come out in packs to beat us. I'm constantly getting death threats on my message machine. Black gangsters from everywhere have put hits on me. I have enough contracts on my head that there's certain neighborhoods I just won't go into anymore.

But I love it. I totally enjoy it. I know you guys hate me, too. A lot of people have tried to take me out, but I'm a real survivalist type. I have people who have put guns on me, try to stab me, and I'm still standing here, so I guess I'm doing something right. They've yet to succeed.

Every culture except for modern-day western culture in the past hundred and fifty years or so has had a caste in society where the warrior was given a position of honor. I feel like skinheads are the warrior class in a society that neither understands nor appreciates a warrior class. So people don't understand us, they're terrified of us 'cause the media portray us as violent.

My Race Is Under Siege

We are violent people because we are so angry all the time, because my kinfolk are being destroyed. The white race is being eroded. And the worst part about that is I'm defending kinfolk that don't want to be defended.

I expect all nonwhites and Jews and homosexuals to hate me. That's a given. But when white people hate me, that really bugs me a lot. I'm obviously not making money doing this. But it's so rare that a white person will go, Damn straight, Steve, you did a good job.

I'm willing to take the persecutions because I know what I'm doing is right. Time and time again I'll see something, like black people will do the exact things that we stereotype them as. The drive-by shootings. You know, typical nigger activity. This ex-girlfriend and I were going to get a burrito, and on this park bench there was this pile of watermelon rinds and we were like, Gee, who could have been here? Total Amos and Andy type thing. Buckwheat would have been proud.

Time and time again people get mad at us for stereotyping Jews as being greedy. I've yet to meet a nonmiserly Jew. I've had so many Jewish bosses who are nasty and rude and cheap. That's part of their culture, but you're not supposed to say that.

Justifying White Supremacy

The reason I say we're supremacists is because no other culture has done what western culture has done. While my ancestors were making cars and televisions, their ancestors were putting bones through their noses. Africans were still making mud huts while the Japanese were making these beautiful silk screens and fine swords out of metal.

The Japanese—even though they're my enemy—I have a lot of respect for them because we should be doing what they're doing. They have it down pat. Discipline. Family oriented. Racially homogenous business culture. They don't allow blacks and Jews in, period.

I really think it encourages mediocrity for the superior to help the inferior. I don't believe in charity, like feeding people in Bangladesh. Feeding them just keeps them alive longer. And they're not producing anything. They're just detracting from us.

The swift should not have to slow down for the lame. Survival of the fittest, you know. If I can evolve higher than you, I'm not going to stunt my growth to help you catch up with me. It just encourages weakness to keep all those starving people alive. People who were born handicapped or retarded are a drag. If a wolf cub is born with some deformity, the mom just chucks it out.

I Come from a Good Family

My parents are very nice, fundamentalist Baptist people. Jerry Falwell was their hero. Honest to God. I was encouraged to send some of my allowance to him and I did. But then, around fourteen or fifteen, I just really thought Christianity was a load of shit and I've been an atheist ever since.

My parents are so all-American it's not even funny. Like about ten years ago, they got into hard-core Christianity and just flipped their lids. Part of the reason I came out so weird and extreme is a reaction to them. I got involved in Satanism, drugs, and every vile act possible in high school. Gee, how many Commandments can I break? That sort of thing. I've done most of them as it is. I'm doing pretty good. I think I've only got two, three left to break.

I remember one time I brought home a skinhead girlfriend. She had a nose ring. She had this leather miniskirt, fishnets, and big steel-toe combat boots. I was totally enamored of the concept of having this woman that scared my parents. Pissing off my parents was totally a kind of a pleasure. I do enjoy offending people. Just because most people bug me so much.

I like to paraphrase that toothpaste commercial: I'm looking for a whiter, brighter future.

SOCIAL ISSUES
FIRSTHAND

CHAPTER 2

Perpetrating Violence

My Dad Helped Me
Confront a Bully

Mikel Jollett

In his essay about being bullied in high school, Mikel Jollett describes how his relationship with his father changed when he asked him for help with confronting a bully at school. Having always been embarrassed by his father's history as a drug dealer and ex-convict, Jollett realizes that his father had advice to offer that he couldn't find in books: sometimes one needed to use force and intimidation rather than diplomacy to handle conflict. After Jollett stands up to the high school bully, he gains respect from his peers and, more importantly, from his father.

When I was 15, I was terrorized by a 12th-grade headbanger. A big, mean S.O.B. who ran with the skinheads, snorted coke before school, and walked the halls with a menacing scowl on his face and a 4-inch switchblade tucked in his vest. I was a nerd. Or, perhaps more precisely, I was an achiever: honor-service-club president, straight-A student, essay-contest winner, track-team captain. I guess all that suburban propriety offended him (hell, it offended me at times), and somewhere along the line he decided that he hated me. He'd sabotage my locker, yell at me between classes, intimidate my friends. He once even slammed my lily-white cheerleader girlfriend's head into a desk. Everyone at the school was afraid of him. I was afraid of him. I had no idea what to do about it.

So, I told my dad. Now, Dad and I were nothing alike. It's fair to say that throughout my childhood, we had a strained relationship. He could be a great guy and all, but because of his ninth-grade education and bad temper, I wanted nothing more than not to be him. He'd been an outlaw in his youth,

Mikel Jollett, "Me Versus the Bully," *Men's Health*, vol. 19, October 2004, pp. 110–112.

running drugs to Mexico, writing fraudulent checks, and spending 3 years in prison. These things haunted me. I mean, they were good stories to tell my buddies, whose suburban fathers were typical rat racers. But I felt marked, the child of a felon, destined for a life of mediocrity. I would literally picture his face as I memorized chemistry formulas at 3 a.m. or rounded the final turn of some track workout, arms flailing, face drawn back in a deathly grimace, driving myself into the ground, running away from what seemed like the destiny he'd created for me.

My dad would've thought this was funny, had I come clean with him at the time. Not because he considered my work pointless, but because he always described prison in the '60s as just another bump on a long road. It was nothing like the modern conception, with murders in the wood shop and gang rapes in the shower. It seemed almost charming, like something out of [the film] *Cool Hand Luke.* A place filled with roughneck, blue-collar guys with missing teeth, who play poker, get in fistfights, and have trouble with the conjugation of basic verbs.

Following My Dad's Advice

Everyone in prison thought my dad was crazy. Whenever someone came too close, he'd go berserk, yelling with that incredibly powerful voice of his, intimidating whoever approached him, convincing them that he was a cannon ready to go off. And maybe he was. In any case, it worked. They left him alone. And he got through it. "I did my time, and they did theirs," my dad would say.

Which is why he seemed like the right guy to talk to about the headbanger. I sat him down one morning and told him about the threats, the intimidations, the months spent with my stomach in knots. He listened intently and thought for a moment, furrowing his weathered brow as I did during geometry class. Then he looked up and said, simply, "Well, you're going to have to kick his ass."

This was a quandary, kick his ass? The thought had never occurred to me. I would have been less surprised if he'd told me to quit school and join the circus. I was not a kicker of asses. The SAT, service clubs, track meets—these things I could do. But kick ass? Absurd. I'd never even been in a real fight. But my dad was dead serious: "Just 'cause he's bigger don't mean sh--."

Half an hour later, I stood in the driveway in front of our house with my dad, receiving instruction, like a heavyweight boxer, on how to throw a punch ("Stay on your toes, keep your elbows in, and when you hit, hit hard"), how to scream really loud to intimidate the opponent, how to duck so I wouldn't get punched. He held a pillow while I hit it, and told me things like "There's no such thing as fighting dirty. Once you're in a fight, win," and "You can confuse him by spitting in his face first, then punching him while he wipes it off." And "Walk up to him with a stack of books and toss them in the air, and when he reaches out to catch them, break his nose with your fist." Like the good student I was, I brought a pad of paper and a pen, scribbling notes in the margin: "Kick knee, then punch neck, yell real loud. Break nose." I was advised to carry a roll of nickels to add more power to my punch. I was told to wear loose-fitting clothes and not eat too much for breakfast. He explained these things the way an astronomer might explain to his son the reasons for a solar eclipse—calmly and with a commitment to getting the details right.

Putting It to The Test

The next morning, I went to school, terrified as usual. I was shaking as I walked down the hall, fingering the heavy roll of nickels in my right pocket. The headbanger found me during the morning break, as he always did—standing by my locker, trying to open it despite the heavy dents he'd made in it previously. He walked up to me and pushed me into the wall. "Hey, punk, am I going to kick your ass today?"

The question lingered in my mind for a moment. I'd spent the morning wondering the exact same thing. Then, slowly at first, I felt the thin, precarious strand of sanity that had stretched and stretched for months—begging for moderation, for pacifism, for the easier route of, well, punking out—finally reach some kind of limit, and snap.

I turned toward him, mustered every frenzied, screeching nerve in my body, looked him straight in the eye—and punched him as hard as I could, dead in the face. I threw the punch with my weight balanced, my elbows tucked, and yelled, "Come on," real, real loud. Just as Dad had said to do.

And then a strange thing happened. I let loose with the most surreal stream of unending profanities that I had ever uttered in my life. I bounced uncontrollably. I screamed maniacally. My entire body, my entire field of vision, every thought, every muscle, every ounce of fear I'd ever felt for the preceding months became pure, bottomless, unadulterated rage.

"Let's go, let's go! I'll kick your ass. Come on!" The head-banger was wearing steal-tipped motorcycle boots and a ring with a nail driven through it. I bobbed and weaved and slammed my skinny fist in his face, 10 maybe 15 times, until blood streamed from his eye, from his nose, from his mouth. It was bizarre. I felt detached, almost calm at the center of it. As if I were watching myself on television. I remember seeing the faces of my classmates, who stood with jaws dropped, wondering how I could possibly be the same kid who'd been discussing T. S. Eliot in honors English only yesterday. They looked terrified. Surely, I'd lost my mind.

Hearing My Dad's Voice

The anger was familiar. I'd heard that voice many times before—that confident, loud, intimidating voice that told you to stay very far away. I'd heard it directed at cars in traffic, at my neighbor when he tried to poison our dog, at anyone or anything that threatened our family. I'd even heard it directed at me a few times. It was my dad's voice. And here I was, having hated that voice for so many years, having resented the life that necessitated it, in the midst of the most terrifying situation of my life, and I was not afraid. The voice had immediately become my ally, just as it had been his.

And then, just like that, the fight was over, the bully left bleeding in the corner. I went home that afternoon and told my dad about the fight. How I'd screamed and wailed and jumped and beat the crap out of the headbanger. My dad took it all in with this enormous smile covering his leathery face. He was hanging on my every word, clarifying details, asking me, What then? What next? and Then what?

Never was my father prouder of me. Not because he wanted me to be a fighter, but because, unlike with report cards and essay contests, this was a success he'd contributed to. It was a sign—perhaps the first of my entire life—that there was a little bit of the old man in me after all.

I spent the next few months as something of a local hero. High fives and back pats and comments in the hallways like "Damn, Einstein, you messed that dude up." Everyone had hated the headbanger. And there was a certain poetic justice to his demise. At the end of the fight, he'd told a bunch of his cronies that he was planning to sic some big "skinhead" on me. Word of this got out, and a number of people took great exception to his, uh, social affiliations. He received death threats at his house and never came back to school again. Last I heard, he was working at Target.

The glory of my victory soon faded, but I noticed a subtle change in my standing—surreptitious nods in the hall, a certain stoic deference from even the toughest kids in the school—which seemed to ignore academic standing and future prospects and instead communicated, rather plainly, that I was a person who spoke their language. I was cool.

Teaching Me the Basics

In the 15 years since that day, I've never once had to throw a punch again. I've backed down on a number of occasions, and have been ready to step outside on a few others. But cooler heads have always prevailed. I guess it's almost always the case that a difficult situation requires restraint, a soft word, diplomacy. But occasionally, it requires a left hook to the jaw. On that day, I learned that, if pressed, I could deliver that left hook. It's an important thing for a man to know.

I suppose that's something my dad always understood. It's funny: I've learned a lot from books in my life, things I resented my dad for not knowing. But as I've gotten older, I've realized that the most important things in life can't be memorized from a book. It wasn't that my dad didn't care about my grades; he was more concerned that I be a good person, with a square head on my shoulders. He was interested in basics.

Since that day with the bully, my relationship with my father has continued to mature and grow. Today, we're best friends. He's sick now, with a host of heart and liver problems that are partly the result of shooting heroin in his 20s. The doctors have said many times that he's going to die. But he just keeps fighting. Working out. Eating well. Trying to manage stress. Again, basics.

These days, Dad likes to say, "I could've been a contenda." What he doesn't realize is this: He was a contender. Is a contender. All that b.s. from his youth never mattered. All that mattered was the attention, the advice, the jokes, the fact that he selflessly gave everything he had to help me solve whatever problem came up in my life.

Because it really is good advice, you know. Whether it's a bully, a tough career decision, a divorce, cancer: "Stay on your toes. Keep your elbows in. Don't be afraid. You may be smaller, but just gather your courage, and when you hit, hit hard."

I Killed My Father

Mark

Despite the media attention given to youth and violence, it is still very rare to hear what children and young adults have to say about crime, poverty, violence, and abuse. In Voices From the Future: Our Children Tell Us About the Violence in America, *young adolescent journalists have interviewed a wide range of youth who have participated in or been victim to violent acts. The oral histories collected in the book are uncensored and each interviewer provides a peer commentary about the interview and what struck them as most poignant about the interviewee's story. In the stark account that follows, a boy named Mark recounts how he decided to kill his father who was abusive toward him and his mother throughout his life. While it is clear that Mark is full of remorse about what he did, he also thinks his actions were justified by his father's abuse.*

That was one of his things—we all had to learn how to shoot when we turned five years old. He made me go to karate and wrestling. My father was very big on fighting.

There was no time for anything except for my father. He always found something for us to do. You could go outside, rake the yard, be done with it, and then you'd have to go sweep the driveway, then go rake the yard again. You had no free time for yourself, no privacy at all. Every day he used to hit me, and one year he molested my sister. I found that out after I killed him.

I knew, even as I pulled the trigger, I was going to prison. I just didn't want my family to suffer anymore, or myself.

My father was hitting me one time and my mother screamed, Freddy, stop it. And so he started hitting her. And after he was done hitting her, he started hitting me again.

There was really nothing my mother could ever do. My mother was going to leave him one year when we were young and my father threatened to kill her mother if she tried to leave. And he would have done it, too. He was that type of person. There was just nowhere for us to go. My father was a very, very powerful man in the state.

I looked up to him a lot because he was a very, very smart man, very powerful, very influential. Kind of made me proud 'cause nobody would ever screw around with him. Everybody was afraid of the man. And nobody ever screwed around with me at all.

There was plenty of times when he'd throw my mother down the stairs, or beat the dog, and I'd want to kill him. You know, the thought would go through my head, but it wouldn't be something I was going to plan to do.

Making the Decision to Kill

About two weeks before I killed him, my mother and I had a meeting with the juvenile officer in the police department. The police knew what type of person he was, but there was never any mention of child abuse from my neighbors, my teachers—even us. They told us they could put a restraining order on my father to keep him away from us. But we laughed at that because that man would have just killed us all that day.

It was December nineteenth, and I had skipped school, and the school had called my house. So I went home and opened up the door, and my father goes, "You skipped school, didn't you?" And he punched me three times and I fell to the ground.

So he beat me for about thirty-five or forty minutes, and he eventually picked up the hammer off the table and hit me in the head with it. After that, I crawled away and I went upstairs and grabbed the shotgun that was on my brother's side of the bedroom. And I walked by my mother and I said, "Ma, I'm going to end this shit." I made the sign of the cross and I asked God to help me do the right thing and I shot him once.

It was weird. I don't want to say he trained us to kill, but in a way that's what he did.

I Threw My Own Life Away

The day I killed him, the cops arrested me. I was put into juvenile custody with the Youth Services. I pleaded not guilty. I was found guilty of murder because it wasn't self-defense or anything since he wasn't beating me at the moment I killed him.

They tried me as a juvenile, and when the eight months of the trial were up, I was seventeen and a half and they could only hold me until I was seventeen in Youth Services. So they gave me six months' probation. And I had to see a counselor for two years.

That helped me a lot. The counselor made me see things in a different way, like if I was to get into an argument with somebody, there was no talking anything out with me. You got a problem with me, then just fight me. Now, today, I'd rather talk it out than fight it out.

It's hard for me to get a job now because I have a felony against me. I got caught with drugs . . . couple of years ago, so that's on my record, too.

I don't think it's right for any kid to take his parent's life, but under these circumstances, I guess you'd have to justify it. But I guess I just won't forgive myself for doing it. I really don't think I ever will. There's the torture that you have to go through when your parents are beating or abusing you. And then if you take their life, it's like the torture that you put yourself through afterwards.

It's your own flesh and blood that you destroyed. I have nightmares all the time. Your self-esteem goes. It's almost like after I killed him, I threw my own life away.

I believe he was raised the same way. My grandfather used to beat him as a kid. I remember him telling me stories about him getting hit with baseball bats and stuff. My father was an abused child.

Understanding Violence as Fantasy

Jane Katch

During her many years of teaching young children, elementary school teacher and author Jane Katch began to write about how young children often play out violent fantasies in her classroom and during play. While initially retreating from these strong feelings and desires she observed in children as young as five, she then started to delve more deeply into understanding what lay underneath these behaviors. In this excerpt, Jane interviews an older student about his cravings for violent fantasies that while appearing at first irrational and frightening, actually seem to serve a particular desire that is not unfamiliar to many of us—the need to be intensely engaged with our minds.

I keep thinking of Jason, in the older class, telling me that while his obsession with violence lasted he thought everything that didn't have to do with blasting someone's guts out was boring. Could Jason help me understand why some of my children love this violent play?

I see him in the hall one morning and ask if he would talk with me more about violence in play. His willingness surprises me. He quickly figures out a time when my class's recess intersects with a period his teacher might allow him to miss, and he is waiting for me at the appointed time. He sits on the edge of the small round table in my room while I sit on a small chair.

"Would you tell me more about your interest in violence?" I ask him.

"You sort of have to wait," he begins. "Last year, my parents and my teacher were worried about my obsession with vampires. That has passed and I got into violent computer games. Now computer games are fading away. It all started when I was little, with Power Ranger and Batman."

"Do you always have something violent on your mind?" I ask. As he talks, I'm trying to understand who it is who "sort of has to wait." Is it the adult who must be patient for the obsession to leave, or is it Jason who must wait for a new one to appear?

"I almost always have something," he answers. "It lasts for six months, or a year if I'm lucky."

"Do you *like* it to last longer?" I ask, still unclear.

"It's sort of annoying," he answers, "when you like something but you only sort of like it. It's sort of hard not to have something you really, really like."

"So you prefer it when you're obsessed with something?" I have trouble digesting this idea. I had assumed his obsession made life difficult for him, with parents and teachers placing limits on his violent interests, trying to convince him he should think about other things.

"Yeah." He leaves no room for doubt, now. "In school," he explains, "I can stop thinking about it and just do what I'm doing. In the car, when my mom is driving me to school, I think about violent games."

Finding Common Ground on Obsession

"Tell me what you like about being obsessed," I ask. "What's the good feeling?"

"Well, if there's something you really like, that you have exposure to, and it's sort of like you really, really like this book, and someone took it away from you, and you get it back and you just have to read it, it's like that."

Now I understand. The only thing better than being in the middle of a good book is discovering a new favorite author, knowing there are more books to explore when this one is done. And what about my love of writing? The best part is being in the middle of a writing project that's going well. Like Jason, I think about it in the car, planning what I'll work on in the evening, or when I get up the next morning. Is that how Seth feels about Deadman?

"Has your interest in violence ever caused you a problem?" I ask, wondering if the problem is exclusively in the eyes of the adults.

"This summer," he says, "I had a major obsession which is still sort of with me. All I could think about was video games. We went to Colorado and we were on the top of a mountain and it was so pretty, it was just the best place, and I spent the whole time reading my game magazine, and that's just like all violence. Well, it has a few strategy games.

"But I don't think my parents noticed. They'd say, 'Why don't you come outside?' and I'd say, 'I'm tired. My leg hurts,' and I'd lie on my bed and read."

I know Violence Is Wrong

"But I know violence is bad," he continues. "When I was little, if someone called me 'stupid,' I would hit him. But now, if they called me 'stupid,' I would laugh and walk away. I would say, 'If I was stupid, why would I have all these friends?' When you're a little kid, you're more impressionable. It sticks with you more. First, you have to know that violence is wrong. My parents don't let me play with toy guns. When I was little, my mom said, 'I'll buy you the action figures if you throw away the weapons.' And we have a TV, but we don't have cable, so we can only watch movies. Now I'm older, my dad is more comfortable with me seeing stuff like that, 'cause he knows I know it's wrong. And he knows I know he knows."

Maybe you have to be old enough to understand "he knows I know he knows" to be able to understand another person's point of view at the same time as keeping in mind your own, before you can enjoy violence and still know you will not act it out in real life.

Survivors and Witnesses of Violence

Witnessing School Violence

Melissa Miller and Cate Baily

*Describing the tragedy at Columbine High School on April 20,
1999 as "the worst day of my life," Melissa Miller recounts the
details of what she observed and felt on that day. Her first sight-
ing of Eric Harris and Dylan Klebold standing with guns at the
top of a hill near the school made her think it was nothing more
than a prank, but when she watched as a friend of hers fell to
the ground after being shot, she knew it was far more serious.
Hiding behind a car until Harris and Klebold went into the
school, Melissa saw them shoot at everyone in sight and even
had a pipe bomb thrown in her direction. After they entered the
school, Melissa ran to the nearest house, contacted 911 and her
parents, and then watched the events at the high school unfold
on television.*

*Reflecting on that day in which twelve of her fellow students
were killed, not including Harris and Klebold who shot themselves, Melissa claims there is no reason to resort to violence to
solve problems. Regardless of the teenagers' feelings of being outsiders at the high school, she argues there are ways to make
yourself belong by joining clubs and getting involved in school
activities.*

In seventh and eighth grade, kids called me names, pushed
me against the lockers, and snapped pennies at my head. I
was miserable and lonely. Every night, I cried and begged my
mom to let me go to another school.

So, I understand what it's like to be picked on. But I can't
understand why anyone would turn to guns. Guns are not the
answer. I learned that on April 20, 1999. That day was definitely the worst day of my life.

I was in the Columbine [High School] parking lot when I heard the first explosion. I thought it had to be a firecracker—some kind of senior prank. Then, I looked up and saw the backs of two guys in black trench coats. They were standing at the top of the hill near the rear entrance to the school. It was Eric Harris and Dylan Klebold. I didn't know their names then, but I'd seen them around. My friends and I would move out of their way in the halls. They scared us.

As Eric and Dylan turned around, I saw that they had guns. I still thought it was a prank. I figured the rifles had to be paintball guns. Eric and Dylan had no expressions on their faces. They showed no emotion—not anger, not hatred.

Then, they opened fire. Bullets struck students on the sidewalk, in the parking lot, and on the hill. My friend Anne Marie was standing on the sidewalk right below them. It looked like they shot her in the stomach. She doubled over and then fell on her back. Her knees flipped to the side. She didn't get up. She just stayed crumpled on the ground.

That was what made me realize—oh, my God!—it was no joke. It wasn't red paint on the ground. It was blood.

A Look of Terror

I was terrified. I quickly ducked behind a white truck. I did not dare look up. Crouched behind a tire, I was scared to move an inch.

Then, a silver cylinder landed about five feet from me. I could smell the burning and see smoke coming out of both ends, so I covered my head with my hands. I didn't know it then, but it was a pipe bomb. In seconds, the bomb exploded and shrapnel rained down on the pavement around me. Somehow I didn't get hit with any shrapnel. Just a few seconds later, there was another pipe bomb, and it came even closer to me. Again, by some miracle, I wasn't hit at all.

Eric and Dylan opened fire again. It didn't sound the way gunfire sounds in the movies. Each shot was like a dart hitting a dartboard. Nothing sounded the way you'd expect. No one was screaming or yelling at them to stop. It was actually really quiet.

A boy who'd been shot in the leg (I don't know his name) got up and ran away. Blood spurted through his fingers as he held onto his wound. Before he reached safety, he looked back over his shoulder at the gunmen. His eyes were so large, and filled with pure terror and pain. The look on his face will haunt me for the rest of my life. I just hope it's a look that no one has to see or give ever again.

Soon the gunfire started to die down. It wasn't Eric and Dylan had stopped shooting. They'd gone inside.

I started to run away. Then, I hesitated. Should I try to help Anne Marie? She was lying there, still not moving. I decided that the best thing would be to get real help.

As the gunshots rang out inside the school, I ran across the soccer field. At the same time, this unbelievable stream of people, of panic, came out of the cafeteria. That's when the screaming started. Everyone was screaming.

To get off of school grounds, I had to make it over a tall chain link fence. Somehow—don't ask me how—I just sailed over it. I was like Xena. The best way I can describe it is that I was on a mission. I was running so fast that I could barely breathe. I thought my heart was going to pop.

Finally, I saw a house with an open garage. I ran in. There was a phone, so I called 911. The house belonged to an elderly couple who let me in and helped me contact my parents.

In a Matter of Minutes, Lives Were Ruined

As I waited to be picked up, I watched the news. I cried and cried as ambulances took my friends, including Anne Marie, away. (For days, I didn't know if Anne Marie was alive or dead.) On TV, I could see my bookbag lying in the parking lot where I'd left it.

I didn't get my bookbag back until June. When I did, it brought back all of my fear. My bag had been trampled on as students ran for their lives. My hairbrush was broken, and all of my books were damaged.

Eric and Dylan ruined so many lives. I know they were outcasts, but violence is never a solution. In junior high, I was tortured. I didn't have the right hair. I had zero friends. But when I started at Columbine, I changed my situation. I joined the marching band and made tons of friends. Now the people that were so mean to me in junior high are signing my yearbook and giving me hugs in the hall.

I found a place to belong. If you're an outcast, you don't have to resort to violence. Join a club. Columbine offers clubs like the outdoors club, the Bible club, the chess club. There are tons of activities that you don't have to be an athlete or the smartest person in the world to participate in. High school doesn't have to be so terrible.

If Eric and Dylan had tried to turn their lives around, maybe 12 of my peers wouldn't be dead—maybe Anne Marie wouldn't be learning to walk again.

A Prisoner's Violent Death

Jean Carbone

While many convicts are jailed because of their violent crimes, they are often vulnerable to violence themselves in prison. In this essay about the death of a prisoner, Jean Carbone, a physician's assistant who worked in a maximum security prison, describes her attempt to save a prisoner from dying despite his fatal stab wounds. Her visceral description of the man's plea for water makes her attempt to save his life even more poignant. Her wish for him after he dies is that he will have found the water that he thirsted for in the last moments of his life.

It was after working hours, but I was still in the prison clinic, reviewing lab work, reading X-ray reports and noting recommendations from specialists to whom I had referred patients. From the clinic officer's radio I heard a call to officers assigned to the emergency response team—they were being ordered to a recreation yard in this large maximum-security state prison. Surely violence had taken place, was probably continuing, and perhaps escalating. I continued focusing on my paperwork, though, because I knew that the response team was well trained and the evening nurse one of the best we had.

Soon I heard the officers rushing in and the nurses gathering in the triage room. Only slightly distracted by the familiar noises, I continued reading, interpreting, planning. I stopped when I heard the triage nurse's insistent voice. "Jean, I need you right away." Now I knew there was trouble.

Entering the triage room I saw a man being placed on the exam table. I saw dark brown skin, prison-green pants, prison boots and, ominously, a prison-green sweatshirt soaked with blood.

Jean Carbone, "No More Thirst," *America*, vol. 186, January 7, 2002, pp. 21–24. Copyright © 2002 America Press. All rights reserved. Reproduced by permission of America Press. For subscription information, visit www.americamagazine.com.

"Cut off his clothes," I said, while pulling on latex gloves; "cut off his clothes now!" The nurses had already unlocked the cabinets (all potential weapons were locked and counted by the nurses three times a day). With large scissors two nurses and I cut through the man's sweatshirt, over his right arm, left arm and chest.

Several wounds were revealed immediately. One was just below his sternum; one was under the right side of his rib-cage. They both looked deep. "Turn him over," I said, so that I could search for more wounds. "Cut off his pants."

I Knew the Wounded Man

"Miss Carbone," the inmate quietly spoke, "Miss Carbone, please help me." It was then that I looked at his unmarred face. "Oh my God," I thought, "I know this man." It broke my heart to realize that he was following the two "rules of respect" I had established in my job as a physician's assistant: don't call me by my first name and don't swear.

"I will help you," I replied.

We worked quickly. Some of us were gathered around the exam table; others stood near cabinets, ready to hand over the supplies that I asked for. "Start a line, no, two lines, lactated ringers, wide open," I said. "Hand me the xeroform dressing, get the E.K.G. monitor on, start the oxygen, get the ambu ready, call the ambulance, hand me a Foley catheter." Nurses, one physician's assistant and correction officers worked to save the inmate's life.

"Miss Carbone," he said, "I can't breathe. I can't breathe, Miss Carbone." Air hunger caused restlessness. The man began thrashing his legs. I was inserting a Foley catheter into his penis, and I was in a position to be hurt by his kicks. The officers—attentive and protective—reached in to hold him down. This caused him even more distress.

"Mr. B.," I said, "Don't kick. This is Miss Carbone. You don't want to hurt me, do you?"

"No, Miss Carbone, I don't want to hurt you. I don't want to hurt you, Miss Carbone." His legs stilled; the officers withdrew their hands.

With the I.V. fluids running, the wounds plastered with airtight dressings, the nasal cannula delivering oxygen, the Foley catheter draining urine and the E.K.G. showing a steady heart beat, I stepped back.

"When's the ambulance supposed to get here?" I called out to the triage nurse. "How long did they say it would take?" This man might bleed to death. There was nothing much more we could do for him in the prison clinic.

"Miss Carbone," he said, "I'm thirsty, give me some water. Please Miss Carbone, why won't you give me some water?"

"You can't have anything to drink now, Mr. B. You are going to need an operation, so you can't drink now."

"Miss Carbone, I can't breathe, I can't breathe, help me, Miss Carbone."

The Prisoner Struggled to Live

The E.K.G. monitor went flat. It was not a mechanical problem—the man's heart was no longer beating, his lungs no longer breathing, his blood no longer circulating.

"Ambu him," I yelled as I jumped onto the table to start chest compressions. "One one-thousand, two one-thousand, three one-thousand, four one-thousand, five one-thousand," I counted, while kneeling in this man's blood. The nurse squeezed in a breath. I continued, but with each compression blood spewed from the wounds in his abdomen. What if the weapon had lacerated his liver, sliced his inferior vena cava, nicked his abdominal aorta? The blood in which I was kneeling became deeper.

Yet his heart started beating again and his lungs breathing.

"I'm thirsty," his quiet voice stated. "Please give me some water, Miss Carbone, please."

"You will need surgery," I said, "You can have nothing to drink." And then, knowing that he was bleeding to death, that he would probably not make it, that he would be leaving us never to return to prison to finish his 37-to-life sentence for murder, I said, "I cannot give you any water now, but when you return you can have all the water you want."

"Miss Carbone," he said, "I'm dying. Please help me."

The ambulance team rushed through the prison halls pushing the stretcher on which lay a man who was not breathing, a man whose heart was not beating. A nurse ran along the head of the stretcher, continuing to bag the man. Kneeling in a dead man's blood, I continued to compress his chest. "No one dies behind the prison walls," was the rule at this prison. "They die in the ambulance, they die in the emergency room, but they do not die behind the wall."

It Didn't Matter Who Did It

Three days later the local newspaper ran the story: "Stabbed twice in the chest with a homemade knife, [J.B.], 28, died late Friday night as an ambulance rushed him to a hospital."

"I feel sorry for his mother," was all I could say to the many prisoners who approached me the next day to thank me for trying to save the man's life. "I feel so sorry for his mother."

"Few would mourn the death of [J.B.]," the journalist wrote. In July 1986, at the age of 18, Mr. B. had robbed a hamburger stand, "forcing a 19-year-old employee into a walk-in refrigerator, ordering her to kneel on the floor, and then firing a shotgun blast into the back of her head."

For the next few days the prison was locked down. All inmates stayed in their cells 24 hours a day while the prison was searched. The murder weapon was never found. A few days later, cars drove up, and a 30-year-old inmate already serving time for murder was taken to another prison.

"Did he tell you who did it? Did you ask him who it was?" I was asked by the sergeant, the captain, the detective, the D.A., the capital defense lawyer and the grand jury.

Who did it? During my failed attempt to save this man's life I had not wondered, nor had I asked, who did it? When it became obvious to me that I was with a man who was bleeding to death from stab wounds deliberately inflicted by another man, my only words were about water, thirst, satiety; my only image was of this man (reincarnated here on earth or living in heaven, I did not know) in the midst of green trees and lush vegetation. He is up to his waist in a pool of clear water. Waterfalls gently cascade around him. He has drunk of the cool, clean water. He shall never thirst again.

My Child Was Murdered

Miriam, as told my Judie Bucholz

In her book Homicide Survivors: Misunderstood Grievers, *Judie Bucholz, a homicide survivor herself, reveals the complexity of the grieving process specifically as it relates to murder victims' survivors. As Bucholz claims, because of the social taboos surrounding death in America, those who are murdered and the families and friends who survive are most often ignored and neglected due to the sudden and violent nature of their deaths and people's own inability to confront their own mortality. In this excerpt, Miriam, a mother of twelve children, explains the discovery of her son's death, the trial of his murderers, and her attempt to find some consolation by working for the support group* Parents of Murdered Children (POMC). *Currently, she works for a prosecutor's office as a Victim Witness Coordinator.*

Miriam is a 60-year-old woman full of energy. She works in the Prosecutor's Office as a Victim Witness Program Coordinator. She is married and has 12 children. She lives in the city and walks a few blocks to work each day. Her husband is a retired civil servant. Miriam has snow-white hair and caring blue eyes. She is very patient and listens intently to what you have to say. She firmly believes in supporting homicide survivors but not enabling them. She explains enabling as allowing the homicide survivor to "wallow in self pity."

Miriam started the first Parents of Murdered Children (POMC) and Other Homicide Survivors support group in the area shortly after her son was killed. Her story is so well known and horrific that to this day people call her from all over the country for help in dealing with their own personal tragedies.

She says she has letters from all over the world asking for help dealing with the personal tragedy of murder. As recently as February 2001, a local television station interviewed Miriam about how she dealt with her son's tragic death.

Her work with homicide survivors and the POMC support group led her to her current position as a Victim Witness Co-ordinator. At first she was a volunteer helping homicide survivors go through the legal process and deal with their pain; eventually she was hired full time by the Prosecutor's office.

He Was Going to a Boy Scout Meeting

In 1985, two teenage boys murdered Miriam's 12-year-old son Raymond.

"My son was 12 years old. He was on his way to his friend's house to go to a Boy Scout meeting together. He was taken off his bicycle, beaten and raped, strangled and sodomized with a broom handle, mutilated, and then set on fire.

"When Raymond didn't show up at his friend's house we went to look for him. They looked for what seemed hours. My husband found him. He was just barely breathing and managed to survive for two days without regaining consciousness. Because there were no brain waves, they disconnected him. He died.

"I remember when this happened I ran screaming. I was the one that stayed home that night while everyone was out looking. I was to stay by the phone in case someone called. I received a phone call from my son-in-law saying that they found him, that he had gone to call an ambulance, and that my husband stayed with our son. I remember just going completely hysterical running from the house to the neighbor's house telling them 'something had happened to my baby and I needed to go there. I needed to go where my husband and son were.' The young man across the street took me to the crime scene. When I got there I saw ambulances and everything and I felt I shouldn't go back there where he was because I wasn't going to be able to do anything while they were working on him except perhaps get in their way and be hysterical. I knew that I had enough sense to know that I would be of no help.

"Then I started hyperventilating. I was lucky that someone happened to have a bag in their car and I think I used that bag a good 45 minutes just breathing in because it seemed I couldn't breathe any other way. Eventually my husband and I followed the ambulance to the hospital.

I Didn't Want to See Him

"At the hospital I kept saying 'I don't want to see him, I can't see him knowing those things that they did to him.' I kept saying, 'I can't see him. I want to remember him the way he was.' At the time they already did the EEG and it didn't look like much hope for him. I was paranoid at that moment. I did not want to see him in that condition. I just wanted to remember him the way he was. Then my husband came to me and said, 'Maim you're going to have to see him.'

"I didn't want to go in the room because if I didn't go in and see him, he wouldn't really be gone. I didn't want to face the reality of his death. But I knew I had to, I had to because they say that people that are unconscious can sometimes hear you and I had to let him know that I was there and that he was still my baby and I loved him.

"To prepare me to see Raymond, my husband had the hospital staff cover my son; they turned him this way [flat on his back with his face to the right], covered him up to his neck so that the only part of him that I could see when I went in was his face. I mean when you walked in to see him you would think he was just a young child lying asleep because he had no bruises or marks on his face except a little scratch. His hair was still beautiful. The hospital staff cleaned him up and you could not tell the damage to his brain by the perpetrators beating him repeatedly on the back of the head.

"I remember seeing the burn marks around Raymond's neck where they strangled him.

"It wasn't our choice to disconnect Raymond; it was the doctor's decision. That really took a burden off of us. The choice was out of our hands. The guilt was not on us.

"It's a horrible feeling to know that your child is out there being tortured and you're not there to help in any way. If I had been there and had been beaten or something else, I still would have felt like I wasn't able to do anything."

His Murderers' Confession

"One of the hardest things I had to hear in the courtroom was the confession of one of the boys. He stated that he was standing watch while the other boy was doing his number on Raymond, raping him etc., and somehow or another my son got away from that boy and came running out and thought this young man would help him, not realizing he was part of the game. He [Raymond] said to him, 'Please take me to my mother. I have to go to a Boy Scout meeting. Please take me to my mother.' And when I heard that in the courtroom, it was just like I had dreamed. I had dreams that Raymond was crying out for me. I think that was one of the worst times in the trial that I had to go through. It was the only time that I had to leave the courtroom because I cried uncontrollably. I couldn't help it. I could not stop crying."

Miriam has 12 children; not counting the children she used to board at her house for other families who could not afford to take care of their own children. Raymond was the youngest of the 12. Miriam talked about how Raymond loved to argue points with her and that she told him he would make a great lawyer one day because of his logical arguments.

Raymond was active in school sports and Miriam keeps his trophies and other mementos in a box in the attic. Miriam says Raymond was extra special because he was not a planned child.

"When I found out I was pregnant with Raymond, it was like 'what do we do? We have all these children and we're poor but we work and we're providing but one more is going to take more away from them and what do we do?' My husband and I considered an abortion and we even talked to a counselor. We discovered that abortion was not in the cards for us. It was not something we could do. We just said 'we'll manage to feed one more' and we had Raymond."

Miriam and her husband made do as best they could for their family and those they cared for by taking on second jobs when necessary. . . .

I Won't Let Them Forget Raymond was a Person

Both Raymond's killers were apprehended. Both had records of assault before they attacked and killed Raymond. One boy had two violent rapes about a year and a half before he killed Raymond. He was sentenced to juvenile detention for the rapes. He was there for a year; until he turned 18 then he was released.

"He was a vicious, vicious person. Before they caught him for murder, he got a girl from the middle school during lunch hour and raped her in broad daylight, 12 noon.

"The other young man, the 17 year old that was involved in Raymond's death was a very vicious and violent homosexual.

"These two people happened to come together that night in the parking lot of a store and just happened to see my son coming in a distance through the field on his bicycle. They decided in just one split second what they were going to do. We should not of [sic] had two individuals out there like that."

Unlike Megan's law pertaining to adult sexual predators, juvenile predators are not required to be listed with local authorities. They do hot have the same restrictions and reporting procedures.

The one killer was sentenced to death row and the other was sentenced to life in prison.

"I have been strength to a lot of people and that is to me is a consolation. If you ask people to remember the victims who have been murdered in the past 10 to 15 years, they're always going to remember Raymond because I won't let them forget he was a person. I won't let them forget the fact he was such a young child and that a lesson should be learned about how we watch our children and our concern about them going places by themselves. Sometimes we think its broad daylight and it's fine to allow a child to go through a field or go somewhere. We are not aware of some of the kinds of animals that are out there and I hate to use the word animals because animals are kinder than these human beings [killers] were."

Miriam believes that there are lessons to be learned from even the most horrific circumstances and once the lessons are learned, they should be shared with others so that maybe they can prevent or ease someone else's pain. She freely shares her experience and the lessons learned from that experience— professional and personal experiences. She advocates listening to and sharing experiences as ways to ease the pain of murder.

I Was the Scene of a Crime

Nancy Venable Raine

Poet and radio producer Nancy Venable Raine was brutally raped in her house in 1985. For a year she was immobilized from the trauma of that experience and her creative writing came to a close. Seven years later while working on a novel and experiencing writer's block, she abandoned the novel and began to write about her rape and its aftermath. In 1998, After Silence: Rape and My Journey Back *was published and the intense response by other survivors testified to its power as a testimonial about a subject that is often silenced or dismissed. In this chapter from her book, Raine draws a portrait of herself immediately after the rape undergoing physical examinations at a hospital and being interviewed by detectives. The strength of her writing lies not only in the excruciating details she remembers but also in her ability to convey emotional detachment and withdrawal in the moments immediately after a traumatic event.*

The only time in the past I'd gone to a hospital emergency room was when I cut my thumb with a straight-edge razor while trying to pry the lid off a can of paint. I was bleeding so badly I didn't have to wait. After eighteen stitches and a lecture about why we have screwdrivers, I was as good as new. This time I was not bleeding. I had soft-tissue damage in my back and arms, but nothing was broken. I had not been beaten into unconsciousness. I was bruised and in emotional shock, but on my feet. I felt like a fraud being whisked past the formalities and a waiting room crowded with sick and injured people.

Yet because a hospital is a place that cares for people, I hoped for comfort and I sensed that the hospital staff wanted to provide it. But for a rape victim the hospital emergency room functions as an extension of the police department, and the medicine being practiced there is primarily forensic.

After satisfying themselves that I was not seriously injured, the emergency room staff began performing the work of criminologists, collecting evidence that might be used in a court of law. My body was still not my own. It was evidence. I was not a patient whose wounds could be sutured. I was the scene of a crime.

I was handed over to a nurse who guided me to a small examining room and told me not to urinate, defecate, wash myself, smoke, or drink anything. She asked me to undress standing over brown paper. Then, handing me a hospital gown, she wrapped my clothes up in the paper. She inquired about my underpants. I told her the rapist had stolen them. Then she left me alone.

The room was cold and I had nowhere to sit except on the examining table. I stared at the metal stirrups with disgust, and then at the faucet over the small stainless-steel sink. My thirst was gnawing at me. It was as if fear had desiccated me. Dust devils swirled inside my body. My mouth was full of sand and spiders. I was alone in the room for a long time with my thirst. Somewhere nearby a man was wailing. More time passed. The man began to scream. My thirst became an agony. I knew the nurses and doctors were busy with an emergency. The man who was screaming was a real emergency. Maybe he was dying.

A Detached Self

The part of me that had split off during the attack was still detached, a shadow self that perched above me like a sparrow, waiting for her dead mate on the sidewalk below to wake up from a high-speed encounter with a plate-glass window. This shadow self followed the ambulance and was hovering just outside my body, observing me and my surroundings with indifference. The continued presence of this "observer," the one that had emerged during the rape, was a misery now. The longer I waited in the examining room, the more frightened I became of this separation. Nothing was predictable. Nothing had sequence. I was a language without punctuation or structure. Verbs dangled at the end of sentences, tenseless. Subjects began to drop out altogether. The observer could read the text, but she seemed to be drifting off, like someone at a party who is pretending to listen, but whose eyes are across the room on the person she really wants to talk to.

Suddenly, I didn't know the person who was sitting on the examining table. I was waiting for something to happen that felt different from what had just happened, but I was still alone, caught up in another upside-down logic, the logic of the hospital that was trying to treat me like an injured human being while re-injuring me, minute by minute, simply by tending to a real emergency—doing the job they were there to do. I did not feel angry at their priorities. I did not resent the logic of the screaming man in the next room. I recognized that I was the one who was out of place.

I felt that the scent of the rapist's rage and hatred was on me somehow, and that the nurses sensed it. I did not resent the fact that with all of their training, skill, and good manners, no one in that place of healing could hug me, even in passing. No one could perform the simplest of human gestures, an embrace that is a welcoming reassurance, a staying-close, a soothing and cherishing that reaffirms a shared humanity. Looking back, I realize that had I been in their place, I, too, might have hesitated, might have sensed the rawness of the spirit that inhabited the violated flesh that trembled before me. What would a hug mean to someone whose body no longer felt as if it belonged to her? In my strange disunity that night, I might not have been able to bear it. I will never know. A three-hour rape exam was anything but reassuring.

In the hospital I felt as I imagine an animal might feel—without words, and therefore without understanding or a sense of sequence. Every emotion was singular and unmixed. I wanted "real" wounds then, the kind that bleed. The kind the doctors could stitch up. The kind I imagined the man screaming in the next room had. I had done everything I could to avoid them, but waiting alone, feeling as I did, I realized "real" wounds could be tended. I wanted them. I wondered who it was that was thinking like this because I felt at the same time that I was dying.

I Had Made A Deal with the Rapist

The rapist had stolen something at the center of what I had known as myself. It was gone with the cash, credit cards, jewelry, underpants, and whatever else he took. All these things that meant nothing to me might be recovered by the police, but how could this missing self be retrieved? The rapist himself might be caught, but he could never produce the woman who had not been raped.

Waiting for care that could not be provided was my first encounter with the world outside the nightmare. I sensed that this experience was a foretelling of all that would unfold in the future. I was cut off, not only from myself, but from other human beings. I thought then that I had made a mistake in calling the police, coming to the hospital. If I kept the nightmare to myself, it would begin and end with me. I could confine it to those hours. If no one knew, no one else could hurt me. Now the nightmare was changing wavelengths, but it was still going on.

I resisted the thought that I had made a mistake in calling the police. I reminded myself that rape was a crime. Rape and robbery and murder were all crimes. Crimes were bad. The rapist was bad. I was good and he was bad. No one can do something like this and get away with it. But I felt as if being raped were the crime because any moment now a doctor was going to come in and ask me to lie down and put my heels in the stirrups. If I had not been so afraid of what was outside the room, I would have run off into the night. But the night was the long hallway where a panther waited. I was trapped in a room with a faucet and all of Boston's water supply within reach, dying of thirst. Alone.

The "observer" was getting bored with my confusions. She was leaving me. There was no place for her inside me. I no longer saw myself from the ceiling, or from just over my right shoulder. I was lost inside with no escape from my inner world, more alone than the ancient hermits who were sealed up in mud cells, never to emerge.

I still had to function. From that moment forward I seemed to become a human water beetle with enormously long legs, miles of legs that held me on the surface of "normal life" in wondrous tension. I could not dive or fly. I stayed out of white water, living on the edges in stagnant pools. I had to move beyond the universe I inhabited with the rapist into an inhospitable outside world. No one noticed I was a water bug. I still looked like a person.

The life I had saved was not, after all, *my* life. I was living moment to moment, slapping down cards as they were dealt. For the first time, I understood my mistake. I had made a deal with the rapist and now I regretted it. From now on, everyone would assess that deal, starting with the police and the doctors and, moving further out, family and friends. What if he never intended to kill me? Why did I believe his threats? Why didn't I have the physical strength to break his hold in those first few minutes? Was there something about me that allowed me to cave in to his demands? Was I a despicable coward? Why had I given in to his hateful needs to spare a life I no longer recognized as my own? The wisdom of my deal vanished the moment other human beings encountered it. I understood it perfectly when it was just the rapist and me in the nightmare in which I was fragmenting and reassembling in new ways that seemed to have meaning. But now that recomposition of being made no sense. Yet it could not be reversed. It had changed me cell by cell. It was my fault that I was alive. If I had fought harder, I would either be dead or be as I was before. Now I was neither. I was evidence.

I could wait no longer. I turned on the faucet and let the water pour into my mouth without swallowing. I washed away his dirt. Then I drank.

I beg the nurse to stand outside the bathroom. While I collect a urine sample, I keep asking her through the locked door if she is still there. "Don't leave," I say. When I'm done, I follow her back to the examining room.

The nurse is taking pictures of my body with a Polaroid camera. She photographs my wrists where the bruises are finger-shaped and the color of dried mustard. She photographs my face. My breasts. My neck. My thighs. She records her findings on a form and puts the photographs in an envelope. My fingernails are scraped, my hair combed over a piece of paper. Then strands are plucked. More envelopes. The nurse then draws two vials of blood.

A female doctor comes in for the pelvic exam. I am not sure I can go through with it. There is evidence inside me. They need it. The pain of the instrument inside me will be worth it, I tell myself. If I hurt some more, they will catch him. When the speculum enters me, I bite my lip. When it opens inside me, I do not think it is worth it.

You're Not A Victim; You're A Survivor

The room is dark. The doctor cuts off the overhead lights and holds an ultraviolet lamp between my legs. She names parts where she has found semen, which glows from its bacteria in the eerie light. I am stunned that she has found semen in my vagina. At first I can't believe it. I had not felt his penis in my body, although I "saw" him pumping frantically on top of me as I hovered on the ceiling. I see the sperm in my mind, the size of maggots. I shudder and feel I am curling up, like a worm that has been cut in half by a trowel. The doctor swabs my anus with a large Q-Tip, although I have told her there was no anal penetration. I feel she does not believe me. Then she combs my pubic hair, cuts and plucks hair. Finally she removes the speculum.

Now she comes toward my mouth with the blue light, I confess. I've destroyed the evidence. I am ashamed of my weakness. She says that's too bad, but swabs my mouth anyway with another giant Q-Tip. She turns on the lights. My skin is purple from the cold.

Then she administers penicillin—two shots in the buttocks and a pill. Venereal disease. Gonorrhea, syphilis, chlamydia, trichomoniasis. I tell myself again that the pain is worth it. Then I think of genital herpes, warts. Then I think of AIDS.

The doctor asks me when I had my last period. I cannot remember. She explains that I should return to the hospital in six weeks—for a pregnancy test—if I have not had my period by then. She gives me estrogen in a high dose: two tablets now, two in twelve hours that should induce it. The doctor tells me the pills may make me sick, so she gives me another pill. If I vomit, I must call her.

I hadn't considered venereal disease and pregnancy when I was bargaining for my life.

I ask the doctor about HIV. She seems surprised at my concern.

"Very unlikely," she says. But she writes down the phone number I should call to make an appointment for the test. She tells me that the virus cannot be detected immediately—I could start getting tested in six weeks. Maybe I'm still going to die, slowly and expensively. I put the number in my purse. The doctor writes a prescription for a muscle relaxant.

"You're going to be very sore and stiff for a while," she says.

"I can't stand to think of all the other victims out there."

"You're not a victim," the doctor says. "You're a survivor. You did something right or you'd be in the morgue." . . .

Telling A Friend

It is time for me to get dressed in the change of clothes the emergency medical technician helped me collect back at my apartment. The doctor tells me two detectives are waiting to interview me. She asks me if I'm comfortable seeing them.

"I want to get this bastard," I say.

"After you've spoken to the detectives, we'll be releasing you. We'll give you a coupon for a cab."

I realize I have nowhere to go. I try then to remember my friends, who they are. I had not thought about my friends before. My closest friend is out of town, visiting her mother in Florida. I ask the doctor what time it is. It is close to eleven P.M. I ask if I can make a phone call from the wall phone in the examining room. The doctor leaves me alone for a few minutes. I get dressed and call my friend Sara, who is getting ready for bed. I don't know how to tell her what has happened. I try to ease into it. Nothing to worry about. I'm at the hospital. No, nothing serious. Well, it is serious, but I'm okay. Wonder if I could spend the night. The couch is fine. Sorry it's so late. What?

I can't say the word. The word is too terrible to say. If I tell someone who is not a professional stranger, the fact will spin out of control, like a car hitting ice. But I need to tell Sara.

"I was raped this afternoon. In my new apartment." For the first time, I feel unable to hold back my tears, but the detectives are waiting. I can't break down.

"Oh, my God," Sara says.

"God wasn't around this afternoon," I say.

"I'll come get you."

"It's okay. The hospital is getting me a cab. He stole my money. . . ." I pause. For some reason it is important to tell Sara something else. "He stole my underpants."

Sara is silent for a moment. "You're going to be okay. I'll wait for you at the front door."

"Promise you'll be at the front door," I say.

I am dressed, sitting on the examining table, clutching my purse. I have tried to be precise with the detectives. I think of Joe Friday. Just the facts. Time. Location. I report the words—mine, his. They have heard them before. I report where he put the tape, his penis, his hands. When I tell them I did not see the rapist, they exchange a look. The woman detective has big hair, dyed blond. Perfectly manicured hands, long fingernails with red polish. I keep staring at her hands while she takes notes on what I am saying. The man is older. Thin. He stands against the door, behind the woman. The woman hands me a card. I am to call them, come to the station to give a formal report. I notice the woman's gun, strapped to her body. I think how lucky she is, to have a gun and such beautiful fingernails. . . .

A Cab Driver's Empathy

I ask the nurse to wait outside with me for the cab, and when it comes, she goes around to the driver's window and hands him a coupon while I slide into the backseat. I leave the door open. "Do you know him?" I whisper to the nurse when she goes to close the door. "Yes," she says. "Are you sure he's okay?" I say. She is sure, but I don't believe her. Still, I let her close the door. I can't think of the name of Sara's street, can't picture how to get to it. I start to get out of the cab, then I remember. I tell the driver to head for Harvard Square. My shadow is not in the car.

I have no recollection of what the taxi driver looked like. When I think back to this ride, I see only a shadow in the front seat. Featureless, the driver was all male strangers, each and every one of whom might be a rapist. The postman. The man walking behind me on the sidewalk. The man sitting in his car at the grocery store. They might all be rapists.

I stared at the back of his head, thinking he might be my rapist. Driving a cab would be a perfect occupation for a rapist. Prey coming to you, rather than the other way around. The rapist could have followed me to the hospital in his taxi, waited all these hours. I thought he could get away with anything. Fear slapped me back into the seat, where I became smaller and smaller. I kept my hand on the door handle so I could throw myself out into the puddles of light left by the street lamps. I was like a coastal island submerged by a storm surge. I had no shore, no definition, no borders.

I said nothing until we got to Harvard Square. Then I told him to head up Massachusetts Avenue.

"Here, turn here!" We sped past the little market on Sara's corner.

"Turn around," I said, weeping at last. The driver pulled over.

"Are you okay, lady?" he said.

This moment is preserved whole in my mind, and still holds a mysterious significance. It was as if I were tuned to a frequency that transmitted nothing but static—the sound of thousands of fingernails scraping blackboards, thousands of metal brushes scrubbing copper pots, millions of bees locked in a metal box—and suddenly, but just for an instant, the static stopped and I heard a single, clear word. For an instant, the woman who had not been raped existed.

CHAPTER 4

Retribution, Renunciation, and Forgiveness

Meeting My Sister's Murderer

Ron Carlson, as told by Rachel King

In June 1983, Karla Faye Tucker and Danny Garrett murdered Jerry Dean and Debbie Thornton in Houston, Texas. The murders made national news due to the dispassionate brutality of the murders, primarily done with a pickax, while the two killers were high on methamphetamines. Both murderers were sentenced to death row in Texas although Danny Garrett died in jail before he was executed. Karla Tucker, on the other hand, became a media celebrity as her execution date neared due to her conversion to Christianity and her utter remorse for what she had done.

While in prison, Karla educated herself, passed a high school equivalency test, and began taking college classes. More importantly she became a devout Christian and dedicated herself to charitable acts. In 1990, Debbie Thornton's brother, Ron Carlson, visited Karla in jail and told her that he had forgiven her for what she had done. After that initial meeting, the two communicated with each other until Tucker's execution in 1998. In the following excerpt from the book Don't Kill in Our Names: Families of Murder Victims Speak Out Against the Death Penalty, *Rachel King incorporates interviews she had with Ron Carlson about his feelings about his sister's murderer, his own views of the death penalty, and his forgiveness of such a heinous crime.*

Ron: When I found out [Karla Tucker] was in Houston, I called over to the courthouse to find out if I could visit her in the holding cell. The person who answered the phone told me that I could request a visit and if Karla accepted, then I could see her. I requested a visit, and Karla agreed.

I hadn't attended the trial, so I had never seen her in person before. I had seen her picture on television many times, and the pictures were not pretty. Karla walked up to the glass, and I was surprised to see an attractive, slender brunette dressed in an orange Harris County Jail uniform. My first thought when I saw her was *I can't believe she is a murderer.* She sure did not look like the monster the media painted her to be.

There were other inmates in the holding cell and other visits going on. It was loud and hard to hear. She said, "Who are you?" kind of defiantly, and I said, "I'm the brother of Deborah." She asked me the same question again, but this time her tone totally changed. "Who are you?" She couldn't believe that I was there. I don't think Karla Tucker or Danny knew anything about Debbie other than she was a witness to Jerry Dean's murder. They did not go to Jerry's house to kill Debbie.

Karla started to cry. I interrupted her. I said, "Karla, I want you to know this, for whatever it is worth, I forgive you and don't hold anything against you." When I said that, I felt like a great weight had been lifted off of my shoulders; I felt like a burden I had been carrying was gone. We didn't have a lot of time, but I could tell that the visit had helped both of us, so I suggested we keep in touch. I gave her my phone number, and she gave me her address. The entire visit lasted twelve minutes.

Learning About My Sister's Death

After meeting Karla, I went to the courtroom to watch the hearing. Since I had not watched the trial, most of what I saw and heard was new to me. Because it had been seven years since Debbie's murder I was able to watch the hearing with some degree of detachment, which would have been impossible at the time of the trial.

There were a number of different people in the courtroom, and I wondered what their interest was in the case. During the breaks, I talked to the other people attending. I introduced myself to two ladies from the victims' support group Parents of Murdered Children. I told them who I was, and I asked them why they were at the hearing. They said, "Oh, we're here for you." I said, "I don't even know you." They replied, "Well, we're here for all of the victims." One of them asked me what I thought about what was going on. I looked at the lady and said, "I'm not trying to be rude, but I don't support what is going on." I calmly explained that I didn't think it was right to have the death penalty. After that they didn't want to have anything to do with me, even though they were supposedly "there for me."

I also met a number of reporters covering the story. Once they learned that I was Debbie's brother, they all wanted to talk to me. A reporter from the national program *Primetime Live* asked me to appear on the show. I realized that if I was going to start talking about the case I needed to learn a lot more about it.

After the hearing I went downstairs to the clerk's office and asked if I could look at the transcripts from the trial. I figured it would be a few pages. They asked me if I wanted to see all of it, and I said yes. The clerk led me into a room filled with boxes that were filled with files. "Make yourself at home. Don't take any of it; if you want to, you can make copies." I spent three days going through the transcripts. I looked at all the photographs. I looked at microfilm. . . .

I finally saw the photograph of Debbie's dead body with the pickax embedded in her chest, the one that the police refused to show me years ago. I felt nauseous looking at Debbie's mangled, bloody corpse. I was glad that Bill and the police had spared me from looking at the picture.

I started to read and became transfixed by what I was learning. I couldn't stop. I took three days in a row off from work and spent all day reading the hundreds of pages of transcripts. Then when I had to go back to work, I went to court every day after work to read, take notes, and photocopy parts of the transcripts. I felt this need to know what had happened. I was thinking about getting to know Karla and making a public statement against the death penalty, but I wanted to know exactly what I was dealing with before I said or did anything.

Everything pointed to the fact that Karla and Danny were vicious killers. The prosecutors had portrayed them both as monsters, which seemed like an accurate description. What I saw was enough to turn any person to the death penalty. But I didn't want any killings done in my name. I believed strongly, in spite of what they had done, that forgiving Karla and Danny was the right thing to do.

It was more than just not wanting to see Karla killed. I would say what influenced me was my religious background and what the Bible commands, "Thou shalt not kill." Jesus teaches that we should forgive our enemies. Of course the bad thing about the Bible is you can read it either way about the death penalty. It is a real hard call to make when you start making arguments out of the Bible.

After reading everything, I confirmed that in spite of it all I could not support the death penalty and that I must speak against it. I appeared on *Primetime Live* and spoke out against Karla's execution. I had never been on television before, let alone national television, but it was just something I felt I had to do.

Visiting Karla in Prison

Soon after Ron visited Karla, she wrote him a letter. He wrote back. They began corresponding regularly, then started talking on the phone. Eventually, Ron decided to visit Karla at Mountain View, in Gatesville.

Gatesville is more than 250 miles from Ron's home in Houston, a four-and-a-half-hour drive. To get to the prison in time for visiting hours, Ron left his house early in the morning.

Ron: Going to see Karla involved a lot of effort and expense. First I had to go through the administrative hassle of getting permission to visit. Then I had to enter the prison, with tall fences surrounded by razor wire and electric gates and buzzing locks. Prison guards carrying guns and cameras all over the place. There is no privacy in prison.

I remember the feeling I had the first time I went inside and the gate locked behind me. I said to the guard, "You *are* going to let me out of here, right?" He said, "Yeah, when you're through you can leave."

Prison is not a place you would want to go. Contrary to stereotypes, it is sure not like any hotel I've ever seen. There is no air-conditioning in the summer and no heat in the winter. There are no pools or color TVs. The only parts of the jail that are temperature controlled are where the guards are, not the individual cells.

In spite of all the hardships, Karla had a good attitude about prison. She made it very clear that it wasn't a Holiday Inn, but she knew that she was there for a reason, that she was being punished, and she accepted her punishment freely. She said that like everywhere else, there were good people and bad people in prison. She talked about the work program that she was in, and she talked a lot about her Bible study. She talked about the other inmates. She was very concerned for their well-being, both physical and spiritual.

We didn't talk too much about the crime because it was too distressing for both of us. I did, however, ask her why she hated Jerry so much. She said, "He destroyed the only picture I had of my mother." I asked her what she meant and she said, "He took a knife and he stabbed the picture with it." She said that they hadn't gone over to Jerry's house planning to kill him, but one thing led to another and that's what happened. It opened my eyes as to why people act the way they do. From what I learned about the whole thing, the reason why the killing happened was simply revenge. And, without a shadow of a doubt, the death penalty is nothing but revenge.

Karla also told me that she wanted to tell me something that she hoped would bring me peace. She told me that Debbie's last words were "Oh God, it hurts, if you're going to kill me, please do it now." She wanted me to know that my sister had called out to the Lord before she expired from this world. To the average person who doesn't know anything about Christianity or about what is said in the Bible, that statement might sound cold or morbid. But it told me that my sister did know the Lord and in her last breath cried out to him. Whatever happened in the end, I know she made it to heaven. . . .

Against Executing Karla

Ron's public statement against the death penalty and the fact that he had forgiven and befriended Karla outraged Richard Thornton, his brother-in-law. Karla continued to get a lot of media coverage, and by now much of it was positive. Both the prosecutor and the investigating police officer had stated publicly that they believed she was a changed person and they liked her. Ron was speaking out against Karla's execution. The positive attention given to the woman who was an accessory to the brutal killing of his wife understandably upset Richard.

As the time of Karla's execution drew near, Ron tried to halt the execution by lobbying official authorities. Ron disliked angering Richard but believed he had a moral obligation to try to save Karla's life. (Danny's execution was not an issue because he died of liver failure on June 14, 1993, while awaiting a retrial.) Ron wrote letters to the governor and members of the parole and pardons board and sought opportunities to meet with them in person advocating that her sentence be commuted from death to life in prison. . . .

The State of Texas set Karla's execution date for February 3, 1998. The case had attracted attention from around the world—some positive and some negative. Many opposed her execution. Her petite, slender figure, freckled face, broad smile, and warm brown eyes caught the attention of millions. Texas had not executed a woman since 1863, and many found the idea distasteful.

Commentators remarked on Karla's "preferential treatment." Some claimed that her popularity stemmed from the fact that she was an attractive white woman. Some thought her life should be spared because she had genuinely changed. Others felt she had made up her religious conversion to gain sympathy. Celebrities, among them Bianca Jagger, took up her case. Even television evangelist Pat Robertson, an ardent death penalty supporter, personally appealed to Governor Bush to spare Karla's life.

Throughout all the controversy, Karla maintained her poise and serenity. On January 14, she appeared from prison on *Larry King Live* and told the world that she accepted her fate and responsibility for the crimes she committed. When King asked her how she felt about her impending execution, she said it was "exciting." King commented on her word choice, and Karla replied, "There's a lot going on, and it's going to affect a lot of people. And it's a blessing to be part of it and to know God has a plan for this."

In spite of everyone's efforts, time was running out for Karla. She began preparing to die. In the middle of January, Ron tried to visit, but the guards refused to let him see her. Karla learned about this and wrote to him apologizing. . . .

Ron: She wrote about having to live with the fact that what she did hurt so many people. "I know it hurts you and him and her children and Jerry's family every single day of your lives—because of *me*. I wish I could take it all back." She finished by saying, "I love you Brother, and I thank you for allowing Jesus to help you forgive me. It brought into my life a freedom to grow deeper with the Lord. *Thank you.*"

For a postscript she wrote that if she were to be executed she hoped that it would bring Richard some peace. She would like to talk to Richard personally to tell him how sorry she was, but she didn't think Richard would want to see her. She asked me, if I had a chance and thought it was appropriate, if I would communicate to Richard and the children what she wrote in the letter.

Karla's Execution

The sun shone brightly on February 3, 1998. Ron woke with dread in his heart knowing that at six P.M. he would likely watch the State of Texas kill Karla. With great effort he dressed and prepared himself for the day. People started gathering in the early morning in front of the police barricade set up outside of the Walls Unit in Huntsville, the site of the state's execution chamber. Television stations staked out the prime viewing spots and set up their satellite dishes. A group of Italian abolitionists sat next to death penalty opponents from the United States. As the day wore on, others gathered.

At first, most of the people congregating opposed the death penalty, but as the execution hour approached, those in favor of Karla's execution gathered, bringing picnic dinners and coolers filled with beer. The scene outside the prison resembled a homecoming football game. . . .

Ron: The execution was supposed to happen at six o'clock, but at six P.M. we were still in the waiting room. We hoped that the delay might mean that Karla had been granted a last-minute stay of execution. That hope was dashed at 6:20 when another guard escorted us to yet another building. We asked him about the delay, and he said that it was "normal." He said it might take another fifteen minutes. However, in less than five minutes another prison official came in to get us and took us to one of the viewing rooms. The state witnesses were in another room.

By the time we got to the viewing room, Karla was already strapped down to a hospital gurney with thick webbing. Intravenous tubes were inserted into both of her arms. Almost immediately, a voice came on over the loudspeaker and asked Karla if she had any last words. Karla turned her face toward Richard and said, "Yes, sir. I would like to say to all of you— the Thornton family and Jerry Dean's family—that I am so sorry. I hope God will give you peace with this."

She then turned to look at her supporters. She said to Dana [her husband and a prison chaplain], "Baby, I love you." Then she said to me, "Ron, give Peggy [Jerry Dean's sister] a hug for me. Everybody has been so good to me." Scanning the entire group, she said, "I love all of you very much. I am going to be face to face with Jesus now. Warden Baggett, thank all of you so much. You have been so good to me. I love all of you very much. I will see you all when you get there. I will wait for you."

Karla licked her lips and whispered a silent prayer. Within seconds she gasped twice and let out a loud wheezing sound as the air left her lungs. Her eyes remained open, and she had a smile on her face.

Her sister, Kari, cried out, "I love you, Karla." Dana said to Kari, "She loves you, too." Jackie Oncken turned to me and said, "She told me to tell you she loved you, Ron." . . .

Karla's death did not end Ron's work for abolition. To the contrary, it increased it. He is helping to start a Texas chapter of Murder Victims' Families for Reconciliation. On occasion, he is asked to share his story; he always tries to do so. . . .

Ron: I'll keep doing this work until we end the death penalty. Besides keeping up my website, I also write to some people on death row. Writing to death row inmates gives them hope and reassures them that they are not alone. There is a passage in the Bible where Christ talks about judgment day, and he refers to those who know him and those who know him not, and he makes a statement about being in prison, "When I was in prison you visited me." What it all comes down to for me is that I just can't see Jesus pulling the switch. I don't think the Son of God would destroy his own father's creation. I just don't think he'd support that.

A Friend of Mine Was Raped

Gerald, as told by Charlotte Pierce-Baker

In her book Surviving the Silence: Black Women's Stories of Rape, *Charlotte Pierce-Baker provides the reader with the cultural and social contexts of sexual assault in relation to black women's experience. Using her own experience as a rape survivor in addition to collecting numerous testimonials from black women, their families, relatives, and friends, Pierce-Baker presents a complex and moving portrait of how black women have survived sexual assault. Additionally, she garners testimonials from black men who are intimately involved with women who have been raped. In the story that follows, "Gerald" relays an honest portrait of his own feelings regarding the date rape of his friend, Dale. When she admits to Gerald that she was taken advantage of by someone she regarded as a friend, he knows she is telling him that she was raped. As a college student, Gerald is well aware of the potential for casual sex to become date rape if there is no consent between the two people involved. Gerald very adamantly argues that black men must become more aware of rape within black communities and they must work at communicating and listening to black women as a solution.*

So far as I know, I only have one friend who is a rape survivor. She told me last summer. She was eighteen when she was raped. I've known Dale since she was a senior in high school—about three years ago now. We were actually involved romantically the summer after I met her. During that summer we spent a lot of time together, and then during the year she just dropped off calling me for almost a year. She didn't even give me a call to say good-bye. So that kinda got me to wondering what actually had happened. After a span of about six months, I called her out west where she lives. She never returned any of my calls. I don't even know if the messages got to her. Eventually she called me; she got my number from the school office last year. We spoke a couple of times before she confided to me what exactly happened. She's fine now. She's active on her campus politically; she's very outspoken.

It was a date rape. She was seeing a fellow who lived around in her neighborhood. Then there was another guy she was talking to at the same time. He was supposedly still very interested in her, but she didn't want to have anything to do with him [romantically]. They were still friends. He was the one who raped her. She just went on a platonic date with him . . . or at least that's what she thought. And the words that she used were, "I was just taken advantage of." The word "rape" never came out in *any* of our conversations. But I know that's what it was. I just knew. I believe we spoke about the incident just that once. She maybe hinted at it in another conversation. It was very uncomfortable. She said she didn't know what to do. There was *no* support mechanism for her there in her town. She was not able to deal with it all, so she just up and left right after it happened and went West.

I did not use the word "rape" with her. But, like I said, I know that's what it was. I knew it was a sensitive issue, and I was not familiar with how to handle the situation. I didn't want to just straight up say, "So he raped you?" or "How are you dealing with your rape situation?" or something like that. I just asked her a couple of things after she told me [about the incident]: "How are you doing?" "How are you holding up?"

Dale had had a somewhat rough life. Her father leaving her . . . and her mother with several children and some of them at home. I know Dale's a very intelligent person. She had some bad things thrown her way that made her into a stronger person. So when she broke down and told me about being "taken advantage of," I knew it had to be serious. That's why I made the connection about rape. She would not have been so upset if it had been something less than rape. I don't know if there are any varying degrees, but for me rape is rape. . . .

When She Told Me, I Didn't Know What to Say

My first reaction when she told me was silence. Complete silence. I think we sat on the phone for about thirty seconds just completely silent. I heard tears in her voice, and it was something way in the back of my mind saying, "Could she have been raped?" At that time she was building up to what happened or to what was going on. Finally she came out and said . . . you know. . . . "And then he just took advantage of me." I don't know what happened after that. Thirty seconds is a long time when you're just sitting on the phone. I didn't know what words to have come out. I didn't know whether to say, "I'm sorry" or "How are you feeling?" or "Where is he now?" or "Who have you told?" I mean, all those questions eventually came out, but I didn't know which ones first to say or how to say them. Should I be comforting? What do I *say* to be comforting? Should I be more demanding—like, "Let me go get this guy"? What does she *want* me to do? I just didn't know. I guess I handled it okay.

I think I was the first person she told. She is not close with her mother, and her friends and family are pretty much one big blurred group of people that don't really do much for her. She might have ended up telling her aunt 'cause I think they're close. But I'm not sure of that either. I asked her how well she knew the guy. She had known him for a few years. After the rape I'm not sure if she got help physically. Later on, down the line, I think she got psychological help. I think it was after she started college. But all this happened to her about two years before she went to college. We used to speak a lot . . . maybe once every month. I haven't spoken to her since the end of last semester. I haven't *seen* her since we talked on the phone and she told me about the rape.

I know rape is taking advantage of someone without consent. But to me that means like *any* sort of roughhousing or sexual play without consent. One person is the forcer and the other is the forced. It doesn't necessarily have to be rough as in bruises and stuff, just something where someone is not definitely down with the situation. I don't know exactly if it has to involve penetration. I would say probably in the legal sort of matter, *yes*. But there have been situations where I wouldn't exactly call it rape, but people have been fondled and caressed and kissed and they didn't want it. I call that a *kind* of rape.

It's More Common than We Think

I know someone who has raped. He's older than I am. He's in his mid-twenties now . . . somewhere around twenty-six or twenty-seven. I know him because I know the person he raped. And I don't know if it's a one-time deal with him. I know that it seems like it might be in his character to be like that. But I don't want to go that far to make an accusation. I don't really know him. And I don't know if he still does that sort of thing. . . . But the more I speak with the women on campus, the more I hear that there is a lot more in this community that black women don't speak about. One topic is lesbianism and the other is rape. I have a lot of female friends, and I've been trying to spend a lot of time with them. In some of my conversations with them they've said, "You wouldn't believe how many people have been raped." They just don't want to talk about it. Rape by family members, rape by peers, rape by professors. . . . And I have no idea who these people are. But these women who are my friends *do* know. But I didn't ask them to disclose the names.

Knowing all that scares me. It scares me that it hasn't been brought to the forefront so that somebody can help. I don't even know if these women have just not brought it out in public, or have dealt with it on their own, or if they're just completely bottling it up. It alarms me that the number they are hinting at is as large as it is. I guess with rape, self-esteem is involved. I mean, I haven't been raped so I wouldn't know for sure, but I can just estimate how hard it must be for someone *not* to think, "Was this my fault? Did I lead him on?" And if they think that it was all their fault, and they bring it into the public's eye and come out with it to someone they don't know . . . then I guess they'd *really* start to judge themselves. "Is that person gonna think I'm a bad person?" It's a self-image, self-conscious, self-esteem type of situation. At least in my personal experience, black women are very self-conscious about themselves, the way they look and the way they want to present themselves—not necessarily more or less than white females, but that's just been my experience. And for them to bring a rape to the forefront, that would really start to hurt them.

Listening and Learning Helps

If I was still interested in Dale in a romantic way, the rape would not keep me from being close to her. . . . But at first I would really want to make sure that she is all right. I would just make sure that she is psychologically and physically all right with herself, as well as against any other standards before wanting to delve into a relationship with her. But I think I'm in the minority of men who would feel this way. For one, I've always had . . . more female friends than male friends. My whole family brought my brothers and me up to be very sensitive. So I've been able to listen a lot more to women and hear what they're talking about than the traditional macho image of a man and how he relates to a woman. I've found myself to be in the minority in a lot of different situations because of that. You *might* be able to have conversations with lots of other guys . . . but I don't know how candid they would be or how often you would hear someone say, "Someone confided in me about being raped, and I handled it like X-Y-Z." You know?

I belong to a fraternity, and we've had date-rape forums. Every year we have hosted a forum with another campus organization. We've had some pretty good discussions. One time we had a large turnout, and the conversation was very candid. We had some role playing where the women and men would act a certain way and then the group was asked, "How would you react in this situation?" "Was she raped?" "Was he in the right, or was she in the right?" "Who was wrong?" It was a good situation. I think one of the most prevalent issues among black males—this is *my* opinion—I never want to speak for the black male race or anything like that—has been that there's always been a gray area about what exactly is "consent." That's really what the black males speak up the most about—settings where the woman will say yes and then act a certain way that's contradictory. You know? How do you read it? How do you judge it? And then it's kind of like a gamble. If you stop, and start to walk away, and she pulls you back as she's saying, "No, I don't want this to happen," and she's pulling you forward and hugging you more and more . . . then that's when the males are like, "Well, why then are we at fault? Why are we the ones that are getting bashed here? She's acting one way and saying something else. Or she's saying yes but pushing me away." That's what's always been the most argued point about date rape with males. *My* one point is communication. It's so important. In the fraternity, we have talked about communication with women, but not about rape itself or how to handle those contradictory situations. . . .

There Are Things We Can Do to Prevent Rape

For me the first step to try to stop rape in the African American community would be to go the churches. That's where I feel that I would get the best cooperation and the most interest from black males. At least within *my* church—it's Baptist—we have a number of black male leaders who are in the business world and the larger community. I see the church as the meeting point—the first place to find people that are trying to take action or at least trying to speak up. At least I would know that they would be in the right mind-set to go out and help others. At the campus level, I guess I'd start to encourage people to set up a specific counseling service for rape victims—a specific service for the black community so that black women and men feel comfortable going to them. So that they're not calling up on some 1-800 hotline for the university and speaking with a random operator about these intimate sexual details. So that they can go to someone they know or go to someone they can at least relate to on an African American vibe and relate what's happened.

There's a lot of gossiping that goes around within the small black family—in the black community at the university. It's so tight, and everybody after a while starts to know everybody else's business, or at least they know what's going on. It's not the same with the white community on campus; there's more of them [whites]. I think there are some differences in how we act on dates and what we expect. I think . . . there is more alcohol involved with whites when they date. If communication is the biggest problem, we need to set some sort of forum in place that can facilitate, that can ease these communications on campus—between black females and males and between blacks and whites.

When I think of black men and women and rape, a couple of things flash through my mind. The first one is the image of the black man's fantasy of the white woman that everybody has about us. If that were true, then you would think that there would be more of a tendency for stranger rape, a black man with a white woman. The other image that comes to mind is the idea of how promiscuous the black male supposedly is. I see now more of a responsibility on the black male

97

to start to understand the statistics about rape and see that this is happening in the community. There should be more communication. Black men need to take action against stereotypes and against rape. We should not leave it completely upon the women's lib movements to say, "We've been raped." We need to say, let's fix this whole anomaly. *We* understand what's going on. We're trying to work amongst ourselves here to bring changes as well.

A Death Row Convict Writes to Help Others

Vince Beiser

In this article, writer Vince Beiser profiles Dennis Skillicorn, a convicted murderer on death row who edits the prison magazine Compassion. *Started in 2001 by death row prisoners,* Compassion *is published bimonthly and includes personal essays, poetry, and visual art, many of them with a religious perspective. The donations raised from the magazine are then given as scholarships to victims of violence. While some skeptics may question Skillicorn's and other death row prisoners' motives, Skillicorn claims it was his discovery of the Bible that has led him to do good deeds.*

D ennis Skillicorn, now 45, was only 19 when he and a couple of friends burgled an old man's house and then blew his head off with a shotgun. He was on parole for that crime in 1994, when, loaded on Schnapps, speed, and Valium, he went on a drug run with some buddies in Kansas City. When their car broke down and a local businessman offered a hand, the trio stole his vehicle and killed him. Skillicorn and one of his friends then rolled on to Arizona, where they robbed and murdered an elderly couple. It's not too surprising that, as a result, he is in a Missouri prison awaiting execution.

But perhaps it is a surprise that, after having inflicted so much harm, Skillicorn is now working to help others afflicted by violence. From his cell, he edits a magazine that recently awarded a $5,000 college scholarship to a North Carolina teenager whose sister was murdered—so that the young man can pursue his goal of becoming a cop.

Compassion is written and edited by death row prisoners across the country. Its eight bimonthly pages are filled mostly

Vince Beiser, "A Killer's Compassion," *Mother Jones*, vol. 30, December 2005, p. 12.

with Christian- and occasional Islamic-flavored personal essays, poetry, and artwork, all of it submitted and edited by mail. *Compassion* has 4,500 readers and has doled out over $27,000 in scholarships ranging from $1,000 to $10,000 to relatives of murder victims since its start in 2001.

"It's not an attempt to extinguish the pain we've created. You really can't do that," says Skillicorn, speaking by phone from Missouri's Potosi Correctional Center. "But it gives guys like myself an opportunity to give something back to those people that have been victimized by violent crime."

Helping Victims of Crime

Compassion raises money through donations from inmates, supporters and its 300 subscribers. Its finances are handled by volunteers at St. Rose Parish in Perrysburg, Ohio, which also helps publish the magazine. But it is the inmate editors who review the scholarship applications, the main criterion for which is having lost an immediate family member to homicide. So far, seven students have applied. "There aren't many who fit the bill and are interested in taking money from death-row prisoners," says St. Rose parishioner Fred Moor. "It's a huge step on the victim's part."

The most recent scholarship went in June to Zach Osborne, 19, whose sister was raped and murdered when she was four. "After many long years of wasted fury, I have finally been able to forgive [the killer] for his crime against my family," wrote Osborne, who is studying criminal justice at East Carolina University. "Through realizing this dream [of becoming a law enforcement officer], I would play a key role in preventing situations like this from ever happening again."

Skillicorn says his change of heart—what he calls his "Damascus Road experience"—came when the drugs finally ran out at the end of his cross-country crime spree. "I was at the bottom, even for me," he says "I decided I could no longer be this person." He was arrested that same day. As soon as he was back in a cell, he started reading the Bible and turned his soul over to Jesus. He's now involved in several religious and restorative justice programs at Potosi. He has even gotten married to a newspaper reporter who covered his trial.

Skillicorn acknowledges that some suspect his motives. According to his lawyer, any evidence that Skillicorn has reformed could only come into play in the unlikely event of a retrial or if he petitions the governor for clemency—something that he may do in the next couple of years when his appeals are exhausted.

Meanwhile, Zach Osborne is proof that the good works of *Compassion*'s staff won't necessarily change anyone's opinion about capital punishment. "I believe in the system," Osborne said when asked his feelings about the death sentence given to his sister's killer. "The jury decided his penalty. If that's what they decided, I guess that's fair."

Still, even some law-and-order hard-liners accept the magazine's efforts at face value. "I don't know how they could be working this for selfish ends. They're coughing up money and giving it to kids," says Michael Rushford, president of the Criminal Justice Legal Foundation, pro-death-penalty advocacy group. "A lot can change in 20 years of sitting in a cell."

After Constantine's Death,
I Wanted His Murderer to Die

Olga Polites

As an opponent of the death penalty, Olga Polites understands that capital punishment does not deter crime and that it is often the most marginalized social groups who are targeted for execution. After a relative is murdered, Polites changes her mind, realizing that intellectually she can view capital punishment in one way while emotionally she views it another way.

I was the one who was home on that Tuesday afternoon in 2000, just having gotten back from a jog. Since my husband was walking in the door from work, I was the one who answered the phone when my sister-in-law called to tell us that her 22-year-old cousin had been brutally murdered in a robbery attempt gone awry. Nearly hysterical, she kept repeating, "We've lost him. We've lost him." After the young men suspected of the crime were arrested the next day, my husband turned to me and asked, "Are you still opposed to capital punishment?"

Since then I've thought a great deal about the death penalty. It's hard not to, and not just because a heinous crime hit so close to home. More recently, lawyers, politicians and even Supreme Court justices are increasingly questioning the role of the death penalty in our justice system. I always thought I knew exactly where I stood on this issue, but now I find myself constantly wavering.

My husband's cousin Constantine was living at home while attending Temple University when his newly moved-in next-door neighbors and their friend broke into a second-floor bedroom window, looking for some quick cash. Constantine who didn't have any classes scheduled that day, most likely confronted them. After what police believe was a short struggle, Constantine was tied up with an electrical cord, stabbed 41 times and shot three times in the head. One of the bullets landed in the kitchen sink on the first floor. When his mother came home from work later that afternoon, she found him. Neighbors said her screams could be heard blocks away.

Going to the funeral, watching Constantine's parents deal with the aftermath of what had been done to their son, was terribly painful. For months they couldn't resume working, saying repeatedly that they couldn't think about the future because as far as they were concerned, theirs had abruptly ended.

He Took Constantine's Life

When the trial took place two years later, all three suspects were convicted, and the prosecutor's office sought the death penalty for the shooter. I was in court for the penalty phase, and as I listened to witnesses testify on his behalf, I was surprised at how indifferent I was to his personal plight. I didn't much care that his family had escaped from Vietnam and that he'd had problems assimilating to American culture, or that his parents had a difficult time keeping him out of trouble.

Before this happened, I likely would have argued that this young defendant had extenuating circumstances beyond his control. But not anymore. Maybe it's because my daughter is almost the same age as Constantine was when he was killed, or maybe it's because the reality of experience trumps theoretical beliefs. Whatever the reason, when I looked at the young man sitting at the defense table, I didn't see a victim. All I saw was the man who took my family member's life.

I find it hard now to resist the urge to support the death penalty, especially since it's getting so much attention. Some states, such as Illinois, have placed moratoriums on executions; others have looked into how well defendants are represented at trial. I recognize that there are sound reasons for doing so. The recent use of DNA has proved that some former death-row inmates were unfairly convicted. Locking up the innocent is unacceptable; executing the innocent is unconscionable. And I agree with recent Supreme Court rulings barring the execution of the mentally retarded, the criminally insane and those who committed crimes when they were juveniles.

My Head Tells Me One Thing, My Heart Another

Perhaps a serious review in the way the death penalty is administered will bring about changes that are clearly necessary. Justice John Paul Stevens is right: there are serious flaws in how we apply capital punishment. Intellectually, I can make the argument that it does not deter crime, and that race and class play major roles in determining who ends up on death row. But the truth is that personal involvement with the horrible crime of murder renders the academic arguments for or against capital punishment meaningless. It was easy to have moral objections to an issue that didn't affect me directly.

The jury verdict for Constantine's killer was life in prison without parole. Although he'll die in jail, there's a part of me that wishes he got the death penalty. I'm not proud of this, nor am I sure that next year, or even next month, I'll feel this way. What I am sure of is that today, my head still says that capital punishment should be abolished, but my heart reminds me of the pain of losing Constantine.

Organizations to Contact

The editors have compiled the following list of organizations concerned with the issues debated in this book. The descriptions are derived from materials provided by the organizations. All have publications or information available for interested readers. The list was compiled on the date of publication of the present volume; the information provided here may change. Be aware that many organizations take several weeks or longer to respond to inquiries, so allow as much time as possible.

Anti-Defamation League (ADL)
823 United Nations Plaza, New York, NY   10017
(212) 885-7700
Web site: www.adl.org

The Anti-Defamation League fights anti-Semitism and all forms of bigotry in the U.S. and abroad, combats international terrorism, probes the roots of hatred, advocates before Congress, comes to the aid of victims of bigotry, develops educational programs, and serves as a public resource for government, media, law enforcement, and the public, all toward the goals of countering and reducing hatred. Publications include *Confronting Anti-Semitism: Myths . . . Facts, Army of Hate: The Resurgence of Racist Skinheads in America,* and the bimonthly online newsletter *Frontline.*

Bureau of Justice Statistics
810 Seventh Street NW, Washington, DC   20531
(202) 307-0765
e-mail: askbjs@usdoj.gov
Web site: www.ojp.usdoj.gov/bjs

The Bureau of Justice Statistics is a unit of the U.S. Department of Justice whose principal function is the compilation and analysis of data and the dissemination of information for statistical purposes. Its mission is to collect, analyze, publish, and disseminate information on crime, criminal offenders, victims of crime, and the operation of justice systems at all levels of government. The Bureau provides an extensive online database of reports, fact sheets, and graphs.

Death Penalty Information Center (DPIC)
1101 Vermont Avenue NW, Suite 701, Washington, DC   20005
(202) 289-2275
Web site: www.deathpenaltyinfo.org

The Death Penalty Information Center is a non-profit organization serving the media and the public with analysis and information on issues concerning capital punishment. The Center was founded in 1990 and prepares in-depth reports, issues press releases, conducts briefings for journalists, and serves as a resource to those working on this issue. Publications include *Innocence and the Crisis in the American Death Penalty, International Perspectives on the Death Penalty: A Costly Isolation for the U.S.*, and *The Death Penalty in Black & White: Who Lives, Who Dies, Who Decides.*

Justice Policy Institute (JPI)
1003 K Street NW, Suite 500, Washington, DC   20001
(202) 558-7974
e-mail: info@justicepolicy.org.
Web site: www.justicepolicy.org

Since 1997, the Justice Policy Institute (JPI) has worked to enhance the public dialog on incarceration through accessible research, public education, and communications advocacy. The mission of the Justice Policy Institute is to promote effective solutions to social problems and to be dedicated to ending society's reliance on incarceration. The Institute has an extensive list of reports and fact sheets on juvenile crime and justice related issues that are available on their Web site.

Murder Victims' Families for Reconciliation (MVFR)
2100 M Street NW, Suite 170-296, Washington, DC   20037
(877) 896-4702

e-mail: info@mvfr.org
Web site: www.mvfr.org

MVFR is a national organization of family members who have lost a loved one to execution or murder and who oppose the death penalty. MVFR members help their neighbors, the press, and policy makers understand the negative impact that capital punishment has on the families of victims and the condemned. Publications include *Dignity Denied: The Experience of Murder Victims' Family Members Who Oppose the Death Penalty, Not in Our Name*, and the newsletter *Raising Our Voices*.

**National Association of Students Against
Violence Everywhere (SAVE)**
322 Chapanoke Road, Suite 110, Raleigh, NC   27603
(800) 99-YOUTH
e-mail: cwray@nationalsave.org
Web site: http://nationalsave.org/index.php

The National Association of Students Against Violence Everywhere (SAVE) is a national nonprofit organization that assists students in starting and operating SAVE chapters across the country. The mission of SAVE is to promote the meaningful involvement of students in providing safer environments for learning. SAVE strives to decrease the potential for violence in our schools and communities by connecting students to safety efforts. The key to SAVE is that it is student-initiated—started by students for students. Information on all kinds of violence related to youth is available on their Web site.

National Center on Institutions and Alternatives (NCIA)
7222 Ambassador Road, Baltimore, MD   21244
(410) 265-1490
e-mail: aboring@ncianet.org
Web site: www.ncianet.org

NCIA's mission is to help create a society in which all persons who come into contact with human service or correctional systems are provided with the care necessary to live their lives to the best of their abilities. The Center provides individual care, concern, and treatment for emotionally disturbed youth, developmentally disabled adults and adolescents, and those involved in the criminal justice system. NCIA is dedicated to developing quality programs and professional services that advocate timely intervention and unconditional care. Some of the publications found online include "Towards More Effective Sex Offence Legislation: Facts Versus Fears . . . Believing Versus Knowing," "National Study of Jail Suicides," and "Juvenile Justice: Facts vs. Anger."

National Center for Victims of Crime (NCVC)
2000 M Street NW, Suite 480, Washington, DC   20036
(202) 467-8700
Web site: www.ncvc.org

The National Center for Victims of Crime is the nation's leading resource and advocacy organization for crime victims. Since 1985, the NCVC has worked with more than 10,000 grassroots organizations and criminal justice agencies serving millions of crime victims. The mission of the National Center for Victims of Crime is to forge a national commitment to help victims of crime rebuild their lives. NCVC is dedicated to serving individuals, families, and communities harmed by crime. Publications include *America Speaks Out: Citizens' Attitudes about Victims' Rights, Violence, Rape in America: A Report to the Nation,* and *Privacy and Dignity: Crime Victims and the Media.*

The National Crime Prevention Council
1000 Connecticut Avenue NW, 13th Floor
Washington, DC   20036
(202) 466-6272
Web site: www.ncpc.org

The National Crime Prevention Council's mission is to be the nation's leader in helping people keep themselves, their families, and their communities safe from crime. To achieve this, NCPC produces tools that communities can use to learn crime prevention strategies, engage community members, and coordinate with local agencies, including publications and teaching materials, programs that can be implemented in communities and support for a national coalition of crime prevention practitioners. Publications include *Designing Safer Communities: A CPTED Handbook*, the online newsletter *Catalyst*, and *Partner with the Media To Build Safer Communities*.

National Sexual Violence Resource Center (NSVRC)
123 N. Enola Drive, Enola, PA   17025
(877) 739-3895
e-mail: resources@nsvrc.org
Web site: www.nsvrc.org

The National Sexual Violence Resource Center (NSVRC) is a comprehensive collection and distribution center for information, research and emerging policy on sexual violence intervention and prevention. The NSVRC provides an extensive on-line library and customized technical assistance, as well as, coordinates National Sexual Assault Awareness Month initiatives. Publications include *Sexual Violence and the Spectrum of Prevention: Towards a Community Solution, Unspoken Crimes: Sexual Assault in Rural America*, and *The Resource* Newsletter.

National Youth Violence Prevention Resource Center
P.O. Box 10809, Rockville, MD   20849-0809
(866) 723-3968
e-mail: nyvprc@safeyouth.org
Web site: www.safeyouth.org

The National Youth Violence Prevention Resource Center Hotline offers information on youth violence and referrals to organizations providing youth violence prevention and intervention services. The federally funded organization is a "one-stop shop" for information on youth violence prevention, sponsored by the Centers for Disease Control and Prevention and other federal agencies. The Web site offers access to hundreds of brochures, fact sheets, reports, posters, and other print publications about youth violence prevention at no cost.

Rape, Abuse & Incest National Network (RAINN)
2000 L Street NW, Suite 406, Washington, DC   20036
(202) 544-1034
e-mail: info@rainn.org
Web site: www.rainn.org

The Rape, Abuse & Incest National Network (RAINN) is the nation's largest anti-sexual assault organization. RAINN operates the National Sexual Assault Hotline and carries out programs to prevent sexual assault, help victims, and ensure that rapists are brought to justice. Information on types and effects of sexual assault, prevention, recovery, and statistics concerning sexual assault is available on their Web site.

Southern Poverty Law Center
400 Washington Avenue, Montgomery, AL   36104
(334) 956.8200
Web site: www.splcenter.org

The Southern Poverty Law Center was founded in 1971 as a small civil rights law firm. Today, the Center is internationally known for its tolerance education programs, its legal victories against white supremacists and its tracking of hate groups. The Center's legal department fights all forms of discrimination and works to protect society's most vulnerable members, handling innovative cases that few lawyers are willing to take. In 1991, the Center established the educational resource center Teaching Tolerance, specifically designed to provide anti-bias resources, both in print and online, for K-12 instruction.

U.S. Department of Justice Office on Violence Against Women (OVW)
800 K Street NW, Suite 920, Washington, DC   20530
(202) 307-6026
Web site: www.usdoj.gov/ovw

The mission of the Office on Violence Against Women (OVW) is to provide federal leadership to reduce violence against women and to administer justice for and strengthen services to all victims of domestic violence, dating violence, sexual assault, and stalking. This is accomplished by developing and supporting the capacity of state, local, tribal, and non-profit entities involved in responding to violence against women. Publications include *Violence and Victimization: Exploring Women's Histories of Survival* and *Sexual Assault on Campus: What Colleges and Universities Are Doing about It.*

For Further Research

Books

Mark Ames, *Going Postal: Rage, Murder, and Rebellion: From Reagan's Workplaces to Clinton's Columbine and Beyond*. Brooklyn, NY: Soft Skull Press, 2005.

Barbara Coloroso, *The Bully, the Bullied, and the Bystander: From Preschool to High School—How Parents and Teachers Can Help Break the Cycle of Violence*. New York: Collins, 2004.

Raymond B. Flannery, *Violence in America: Coping With Drugs, Distressed Families, Inadequate Schooling, and Acts of Hate*. New York: Continuum International Publishing Group, 2000.

Cybelle Fox, David J. Harding, Jal Mehta, and Wendy Roth, *Rampage: The Social Roots of School Shootings*. New York: Basic Books, 2002.

James Gilligan, *Preventing Violence*. New York: Thames and Hudson, 2001.

Henry Giroux, *Fugitive Cultures: Race, Violence, and Youth*. New York: Routledge, 1996.

Rachel King, *Don't Kill in Our Names: Families of Murder Victims Speak Out Against the Death Penalty*. New Brunswick, NJ: Rutgers University Press, 2003.

Jack Levin and Gordana Rabrenovic, *Why We Hate*. Amherst, NY: Prometheus Books, 2004.

Charlotte Pierce-Baker, *Surviving the Silence: Black Women's Stories of Rape*. New York: W.W. Norton & Co., 1998.

Rachel Simmons, *Odd Girl Out: The Hidden Culture of Aggression in Girls*. Orlando: Harvest Books, 2003.

Periodicals

George M. Anderson, "Healing the Wounds of Murder: Among the victims are family members of both the murdered and the murderer," *America*, July 30, 2001.

Aimee Lee Ball, "She's Come Undone," *O, The Oprah Magazine*, September 2004.

Vince Beiser, "Vengeance is Mom's," *Mother Jones*, March–April 2006.

Michael Blanding, "Growing Up in Gangland," *Boston Magazine*, January 2004.

Alfred Blumstein, "Youth, Guns, and Violent Crime," *The Future of Children*, Summer–Fall 2002.

Raymond Bonner and Ford Fressenden, "States With No Death Penalty Share Lower Homicide Rates," *New York Times*, September 22, 2000.

Cory A. Booker, "No. 003 The New City: Ladies and Gentlemen, Welcome to Newark, New Jersey," *Esquire*, October 2006.

Daniel Duane, "Straight Outta Boston: Why Is the 'Boston Miracle'—the Only Tactic Proven to Reduce Gang Violence—Being Dissed by the L.A.P.D., the FBI, and Congress?," *Mother Jones*, January–February 2006.

Ebony, "The Truth about Date Rape," September 1997.

Mary Gaitskill, "On Not Being a Victim: Sex, Rape, and the Trouble with Following Rules," *Harper's*, March 1994.

Thom Gillespie, "Violence, Games & Art (Part 2)," *Technos: Quarterly for Education and Technology*, Summer 2000.

Carolyn Kleiner, "Breaking the Cycle, (No More Victims Works to Keep Children of Criminals out of Prison)," *U.S. News & World Report*, April 29, 2002.

Kathiann M. Kowalski, "Violence Hits Hard: Violence Against Teens Can Have Devastating Consequences. Find Out What They Are and What You Can Do," *Current Health 2*, March 2004.

Adrian Nicole LeBlanc, "The Outsiders," *The New York Times Magazine*, August 22, 1999.

Eli Lehrer, "Hell Behind Bars: The Crime that Dare Not Speak Its Name," *National Review*, February 5, 2001.

Samantha Levine, "The Perils of Young Romance," *U.S. News & World Report*, August 13, 2001.

Cindy D. Ness, "The Rise in Female Violence," *Daedalus*, Winter 2007.

off our backs, "What It Would Really Take to End Rape?," September–October 2002.

Jeninne Lee St. John, "A Road Map to Prevention," *Time*, March 26, 2007.

Isis Sapp-Grant and Rosemarie Robotham, "Gang Girl: The Transformation of Isis Sapp-Grant," *Essence*, August 1998.

Polly Sparling, "Mean Machines: New Technologies Let the Neighborhood Bully Taunt You Anywhere, Anytime. But You Can Fight Back," *Current Health 2*, September 2004.

Karen Wright, "Guns, Lies, and Video: Does Violent TV Breed Violence? Do Video Games Breed More of It?," *Discover*, April 2003.

Index

A

Abuse
  fight against, 32, 110, 111
  forms of, 12–13
  violence caused by, 14, 47–50
Acquaintance rape, 12, 91–98
African Americans. See Black
  people
After Silence: Rape and My Journey
  Back (Raine), 70
Aggravated assault, statistics, 12
  See also Rape; Sexual assault
Alcohol, violence caused by, 97, 99
Anger
  controlling, 28, 44–45, 46
  violence caused by, 15, 37, 72
Anti-Defamation League (ADL),
  105
Anti-Semitism, fight against, 105
Assault, statistics, 12
  See also Rape; Sexual assault

B

Baily, Cate, 55
Behavior, transforming, 15–16, 81,
  87, 100–101
Beiser, Vince, 99
Belonging, 55, 58
Bible, 84, 86, 90, 99, 101
Bigotry, 32–39, 105, 110
Black people
  dealing with rape, 91–98
  violence against, 36–38
  See also Race
Brutality, 65, 81, 84
Bucholz, Judie, 64

Bullying, 12–15, 23, 32–35, 41–46,
  55, 58
Bureau of Justice Statistics, 105–
  106

C

Canada, Geoffrey, 18–28
Capital punishment. See Death
  penalty
Carbone, Jean (witness), 59–63
Carlson, Ron (survivor), 81–90
Centers for Disease Control and
  Prevention, 109
Children
  abuse of, 47–50
  of convicts, 41–42
  murders of, 13, 64–69
  violence against, 12, 19
  violence prevention efforts for,
    29–31
  violent fantasies of, 51–53
  See also Families; Youth
Christianity, 86, 90
  conversion to, 81, 87, 100–101
  reaction against, 38–39
Churches, violence prevention
  efforts, 96–98
Cities, violence in, 18–28
Class divisions
  death penalty and, 104
  violence caused by, 13, 15
Club BADDD, 30–31
Codes of conduct, 18–28
Colleges. See Schools
Columbine High School (CO)
  massacre, 13, 14–15, 55–58

Communication, violence prevention by, 91–98

Communities, violence prevention efforts of, 15–16, 96–98, 107, 108–109

Compassion (prison magazine), 99–101

Conflict resolution, 41, 46, 49, 58

Contreras, Gabriela (witness), 29–31

Convicts
death row, 89–90, 99–104
violence among, 59–63

Counseling, prevention through, 15, 35, 49, 97

Crimes
causes of, 13–15
hate, 36
prevention of, 15–16, 108–109
statistics on, 12, 15, 105–106
youth, 104, 106
See also Murder; Rape; Violence

Criminal justice system, 106, 108, 110
See also Police

Criminally insane, execution of, 104

D

Dancers, male, violence against, 32–35

Date rape, 91–98, 111

Dean, Jerry (victim), 81–82, 85–86, 87, 88

Death
conditioning for, 18–19
taboos, 64

Death penalty
opposition to, 81–90, 106–107
support for, 101, 102–104

Death Penalty Information Center (DPIC), 106

Derogatory comments, 12–13

Detachment, as response to violence, 70–79, 82

Diplomacy, 41, 46, 49

Disability
treatment of, 108
violence based on, 12–13, 38

Discrimination, fight against, 110
See also Prejudice

DNA, 104

Domestic abuse, 12, 47–50, 111

Drugs, violence caused by, 29–30, 81, 99, 100

E

Economic disparities, violence caused by, 13, 15

Education, 14, 15, 110

Emotional illness, treatment of, 108

Emotions, controlling, 27–28

Everyday life, violence in, 12–16, 18–39

F

Families
abuse in, 47–50, 94
of murder victims, 64–69, 81–90, 102–104, 106–107
See also Children; Parents

Fantasies, violent, 51–53

Fear, 25, 79
controlling, 20–22, 28, 43–45
culture of, 14

Feminist theories of violence, 15

Fighting, 19, 20, 29–30

Fist Stick Knife Gun: A Personal History of Violence in America (Canada), 18

Forgiveness, 81–90, 100

    See also Reconciliation

Friends, support from, 77–78, 91–98

    See also Survivors

G

Gang violence, 29–31, 36

Garrett, Danny (murderer), 81, 82, 84, 86

Gender, violence based on, 12–13, 15

Gerald (friend of rape victim), 91–98

Ghettos, violence in, 18–28

Gold, Rhee (survivor), 32–35

Great Britain, violence in, 36

Grieving, 64

H

Handguns, 19, 20

Harassment, 13, 14–15, 23, 32–35, 55, 58

Harris, Eric (murderer), 13, 14–15, 55–58

Hatred

    fight against, 105, 110

    violence caused by, 36–39, 72

High schools. *See* Columbine High School (CO) massacre; Schools

Homes, violence in, 12, 13

    See also Families

Homosexuals, violence against, 12–13, 32–35, 36, 37

Hospitals, care of rape victims, 70–78

Human services. *See* Social services

I

Incarceration. *See* Convicts; Prisons

Incest, fight against, 110

Inequalities, violence caused by, 13–15

Innocent people, convictions of, 104

Intimidation tactics, 12–13, 41, 43–45

J

Japanese people, 38

Jesus Christ, 90, 101

Jewish people, violence against, 36–38, 105

Jollett, Mikel, 41–46

Justice Policy Institute (JPI), 106

K

Katch, Jane, 51

King, Rachel, 81

Klebold, Dylan (murderer), 13, 14–15, 55–58

Knife fighting, 20

Koeniger, Kevin (witness), 13

L

Life, everyday, violence in, 12–16, 18–39

Listening, violence prevention by, 91–98

Littleton (CO) shootings. *See* Columbine High School (CO) massacre

M

Manhood, 20, 32–35

Mark (murderer), 47–50

Megan's law, 68

Men
> black, 91–98
> violence among, 15
> *See also* Young men

Mental illness
> treatment of, 108
> violence caused by, 14, 28

Mentally retarded, execution of, 104

Methamphetamines, violence caused by, 81

Miller, Melissa (witness), 55–58

Minds, engagement of, 51–53

Miriam (survivor), 64–69

Murder Victims' Families for Reconciliation (MVFR), 106–107

Murders
> causes of, 18–19, 86
> personal accounts of, 47–50, 99–101
> in prison, 59–63
> statistics on, 12
> survivors of, 64–69, 81–90, 102–104, 106–107

N

National Association of Students Against Violence Everywhere (SAVE), 107

National Center for Victims of Crime (NCVC), 108

National Center on Institutions and Alternatives (NCIA), 107–108

National Crime Prevention Council, 108–109

The National Sexual Assault Hotline, 110

National Sexual Violence Resource Center (NSVRC), 109

National Youth Violence Prevention Resource Center, 109

Neglect, violence caused by, 14

O

Obsessions, violent, 51–53

Office on Violence Against Women (OVW), 110–111

Osborne, Zach (survivor), 100, 101

P

Parents
> murder of, 47–50
> support from, 41–46
> violence as reaction to, 38–39
> *See also* Children; Families

Parents of Murdered Children (POMC), 64, 65, 83

Peer pressure, 32

Physical abuse, 14, 32

Pierce-Baker, Charlotte, 91

Play, aggressive, 12, 94

Police, 73–74, 77–78

Polites, Olga (survivor), 102–104

Poor people, violence against, 12

Populations, vulnerable, 12, 104

Poverty, violence caused by, 14, 19

Prejudice, 32–39, 110

Prevention efforts, 20, 49
> communication as, 91–98
> community, 15–16, 96–98, 107, 108–109
> school, 15–16, 29–31, 35, 97, 107

Prisons, 84–85, 89–90, 106, 107–108
> violence in, 12, 42, 59–63
> *See also* Convicts

Property, defending, 18–19, 26, 27

Punishment. *See* Criminal justice system; Death penalty; Prisons

R

Race
death penalty and, 104
violence based on, 12–13, 36–38
Raine, Nancy Venable (survivor), 70–79
Rape
prevention, 96–98, 110
statistics, 12
survivors, 70–79, 91–98
Rape, Abuse & Incest National Network (RAINN), 110
Rapists, 72–74, 78–79, 94, 110
Reconciliation, 81–90, 99–101, 106–107
Reggae culture, 36
Religion, 84, 99
See also Christianity
Remorse, 81, 87, 88, 89
Repeat offenders, 68, 99
Reputation, defending, 18–19
Restitution, 99–101
Retribution, 102–104
See also Death penalty
Revenge, violence caused by, 15, 86
Robbery, 73
Role models, 18–28
Rude boy culture, 36
Rules of the street, 18–28
Rusch, Elizabeth, 29

S

Schools
violence in, 12, 13, 55–58, 94

violence prevention efforts in, 15–16, 29–31, 35, 97, 107
See also Columbine High School (CO) massacre
Self-esteem, 50, 95
Sexual abuse, violence caused by, 14, 47–48
Sexual assault, 14, 65
prevention, 109, 110–111
See also Rape
Sexual predators, 68
Sexual preference, violence based on, 12–13, 32–35, 36, 37
Shame, violence caused by, 14, 25
Silence: Black Women's Stories of Rape (Pierce-Baker), 91
Skillicorn, Dennis (murderer), 99–101
Skinheads, 36–39, 45
Social hierarchies
death penalty and, 102, 104
violence caused by, 13, 15
Social services, 15, 30, 107–108
South Bronx (NY), violence in, 18–28
Southern Poverty Law Center, 110
Stalking, 12, 111
Stereotyping, 36, 37, 97–98
Stevens, John Paul (Supreme Court Justice), 104
Storm Trooper Steve (skinhead), 36–39
Stranger rape, 97
Streets, survival on, 18–28
Supreme Court, death penalty views, 104
Survivors
assistance to, 99–101
personal accounts of, 18–28, 64–98, 102–104
See also Victims

T

Teaching Tolerance, 110
Teasing, 12–14, 23
Terrorism, fight against, 105
Thornton, Debbie (victim), 81–82, 83, 86
Thornton, Richard (survivor), 86, 88, 89
Threats, 12–13, 41, 43–45
Tolerance, 15–16, 110
Trauma, responses to, 70–79
Trench coat mafia, 13
　　See also Harris, Eric; Klebold, Dylan
Tucker, Karla Faye (murderer), 82, 84–86
　　execution of, 81, 84, 86–90
Turf, defending, 18–19, 26, 27

U

United States
　　crime rates, 12, 15
　　violence in, 36
Universities. *See* Schools
U.S. Department of Justice, 105–106, 110–111

V

Verbal abuse, violence caused by, 12–13
　　See also Teasing; Threats
Victims
　　assistance to, 99–101, 108, 110–111
　　information on, 105–106
　　personal accounts of, 70–79
　　self-blame from, 13–14, 74–76, 95
　　support for, 83, 91–98
　　See also Survivors

Video games, violent, 52, 53
Violence
　　causes of, 13–15, 72, 81, 86, 97, 99–100
　　conflict resolution by, 41, 58
　　in everyday life, 12–16, 18–39
　　fantasies of, 51–53
　　forms of, 12–13
　　perpetrating, 41–53
　　school, 12, 13, 55–58, 94
　　statistics on, 12, 15
　　witnessing, 55–63
　　workplace, 12, 13, 15–16
　　youth, 13, 14–15, 36–39, 41–46
　　See also Crimes; Prevention; *and specific forms of violence*
Voices From the Future: Our Children Tell Us About the Violence in America, 47

W

War, as conditioning for violence, 19
Weapons, 19, 20
White people, violence among, 97
White supremacists, 36–39, 110
Withdrawal, as response to violence, 70–79
Witnesses, 55–63
Women
　　black, 91–98
　　violence against, 12, 14, 47–48, 110–111
　　See also Rape
Working-class, violence among, 36
Workplaces
　　violence in, 12, 13
　　violence prevention efforts in, 15–16

Y

Young men
bonds between, 18–28
perpetrating violence in, 14,
41–50, 68
violence against, 12, 32–35
See also Harris, Eric; Klebold,
Dylan; Storm Trooper Steve

Youth
crime among, 104, 106
violence among, 13, 14–15,
36–39, 41–46
violence prevention efforts
among, 29–31, 109
See also Children